D0571912

HELLO WORLD!

A PERSONAL MESSAGE TO THE BODY OF CHRIST

PAUL F. CROUCH, SR.

Hallelujah! I want to express publicly before His people my heartfelt thanks to God for His mighty miracles. All who are thankful should ponder them with me. For His miracles demonstrate His honor, majesty, and eternal goodness. (PSALM 111:1–3 TLB)

THOMAS NELSON PUBLISHERS®
Nashville

A Division of Thomas Nelson, Inc.
www.ThomasNelson.com

Copyright © 2003 by Paul F. Crouch, Sr.

All rights reserved. Written permission must be secured from the publisher to use or reproduce any part of this book, except for brief quotations in critical reviews or articles.

Published in Nashville, Tennessee, by Thomas Nelson, Inc.

Unless otherwise noted, all Scripture quotations are from THE KING JAMES VERSION.

Scripture quotations noted TLB are from *The Living Bible,* copyright © 1971. Used by permission of Tyndale House Publishers, Inc., Wheaton, Illinois 60189. All rights reserved.

Scripture quotations noted NKJV are from THE NEW KING JAMES VERSION. Copyright © 1979, 1980, 1982, Thomas Nelson, Inc., Publishers.

Scripture quotations noted NASB are from the NEW AMERICAN STANDARD BIBLE®, © Copyright The Lockman Foundation 1960, 1962, 1963, 1968, 1971, 1972, 1973, 1975, 1977. Used by permission.

Library of Congress Cataloging-in-Publication Data

Crouch, Paul F.
   Hello, world! : a personal message to the Body of Christ / Paul F. Crouch, Sr.
   p. cm.
   Rev. ed. of: I had no father but God. c1993.
   ISBN 0-7852-6274-1 (pbk.)
   1. Trinity Broadcasting Network--History. 2. Crouch, Paul F. I. Crouch, Paul F.
I had no father but God. II. Title.
   BV656.3.C76 2003
   269'.2'092—dc21   2002156567

ISBN: 62342NRM (hc)
ISBN: 63128NRM (pb)
ISBN: 0-7852-6274-1 (pb)

Printed in the United States of America
03 04 05 06 07 — 10 9 8 7 6 5 4 3 2 1

I lovingly dedicate this book to my two sons,

Paul Franklin Crouch, Jr. and Matthew Wendell Crouch

and to my children's children,

Brandon Paul Crouch,
Brittany Brianne Crouch,
Carra Linda Crouch,
Matthew Caylan Crouch,
and Cody Andrew Crouch,

and to their mother, Janice Bethany Crouch, who gave them to me.

I also dedicate this book to all my sons and daughters within the Body of Christ who, through the years, have labored side by side with Jan and me to raise up this mighty voice—God's voice to all the world.

O God, you have helped me from my earliest childhood—and I have constantly testified to others of the wonderful things you do. And now that I am old and gray, don't forsake me. Give me time to tell this new generation (and their children too) about all your mighty miracles. (Psalm 71:17–18 TLB)

TO MY TWO SONS

It came from your Father,
It was all he had to give,
So it's yours to use and cherish
As long as you may live.
If you lose the watch he gave you
It can always be replaced,
But a black mark on your name, son,
Can never be erased.
It was clean the day you took it
And a worthy name to bear,
When I got it from my father
There was no dishonor there.
So make sure you guard it wisely . . .
After all is said and done,
You'll be glad the name is spotless
When you give it to your son.
(Author Unknown)

CONTENTS

FOREWORD

BY DR. JACK W. HAYFORD

He who is not against us is on our side.
(Mark 9:40 NKJV)

YOU HAVE JUST OPENED A VOLATILE BOOK—ONE that holds some highly explosive, combustible material. This introduction is a warning. Not a warning to lay it down, but to let its contents work. Let me explain.

Paul Crouch called me: "Pastor, Jan and I felt we would like you to read my new book and raise questions, make suggestions, or give me correction. It will be going to the printers in a few days—I know you're busy, but would you . . . ?"

I was unhesitating and immediate. "Absolutely, Paul!"

My schedule had never been more full, time never more precious, but I knew I needed to do it for two reasons. First, because Paul was appealing to me as his pastor, and second, because he had added that he was writing very forthrightly about a number of people involved and many of the struggles he'd undergone during the thirty years since he founded Trinity Broadcasting Network.

As for the first reason, I felt a holy obligation under Christ to serve his request if I could. Paul and Jan have referred to me as "Pastor" in a personal sense for many years, but it's likely that most people wouldn't know the nature of that relationship. In the pages of the story that follow, Paul tells how it began, so I'll leave that part of it to him. What he doesn't tell is how God dealt with me about them—Paul and Jan—and how that dealing affected my feelings toward the whole Body of Christ.

I had not met them yet on that day nearly thirty years ago. When I walked into the den at our house, no one was in the room, but the television was on, and the Crouches were there on the screen. I'd seen their broadcast a few times—sent from a single small station somewhere down in Orange County, California, about sixty miles away from The Church On The Way, where I have now pastored for more than a quarter century.

Pardon my frankness (many of you have heard me tell this over TV before), but as I gazed at the screen I was inwardly irritated. It wasn't anything that was said, it was simply that the Crouches didn't suit my taste. Everything seemed so overdone—from their style, to the set, to Paul's suit and Jan's makeup. Though I had my opinion, I was Christian enough not to have ever spoken anything against them, but not enough to recognize the subtlety of the Adversary's spirit of judgmentalism that had crept into my soul. As I moved toward the TV set to turn the switch off, a gentle but probing voice whispered within my heart: *"You don't approve of the way I created them, do you?"*

I was stopped in my tracks; stunned by the sudden awareness of the facts that God Almighty Himself had been monitoring my soul and that He now stepped forward to make a very pointed correction.

To describe my response could sound overdone in its own way, were I to attempt a complete description of what followed. But I had instantaneously been smitten with such conviction for the smallness of my soul, I could hardly walk. I stumbled from the den to the living room, crumpled to my knees there, and then prostrated myself on the floor—alone before God . . . and weeping. Without elaborating on my prayer, it's enough to say that I recognized the horrible way our humanity is tempted—certainly mine!—to "sit in judgment on the Creator's unique workings in different ones of His sons and daughters." I suddenly saw that this was the same spirit that rose within Lucifer when he said, "I will be as God," for he was essentially presuming the right to create beings in *his* image. I wept, perceiving the awfulness of the lie veiled in any human notion that *"people ought to be like I think they should be"*; the blind-minded idea that it was *my* business to disapprove of any who didn't fit *my* preferences—*my* image! And then, with tears, I recanted any claim to give place *ever* again to such sinful arrogance.

Let me hasten to say that God did *not* impress me with the idea that everything Paul and Jan Crouch did was flawless or perfect in His sight. He simply asserted that they were HIS—by His creative right as their Maker and by His redeeming purchase and call in Christ. He removed them from the circle of my judgment and moved them into the circle of my love. And though we still had never met, I instantly felt a heart-humbling and loving commitment to them as their brother in Jesus our Lord.

Through this experience, I began to discover how impacting

this same attitude had been on my feeling toward other leaders in the Body of Christ, as well as people of marked difference from myself, whether renowned or not. As I yielded to the Holy Spirit, my heart began to change—dramatically. I decided to pay the price—and there *is* one—of seeking to always live within Jesus' words, even when some may not understand that decision; the words: "He who is not against us is on our side." My understanding had been quickened by His Spirit, and I now realized I was to steadfastly resist the intrusion of an "adversary spirit" into my attitudes; a spirit that pervades the mind-set of Christians more than is generally recognized.

An adversary spirit, to my understanding, is one that is bound to separate, divide, and criticize other Christians, and always for self-justifying reasons—that is, reasons that you and I may think right, proper, or worthy. It may be over doctrinal differences (not *error*), which *should* be judged, but *emphasis,* which may be unique to the individual; or such attitudes may simply run from disapproval or distaste for an individual's personality, style, and mannerisms to their church affiliation or any of the numerous other things that distinguish each of us from one another.

I eventually came to learn that to refuse the adversary spirit can bring you under the judgment of others, simply because you refuse to make *their* enemies *yours!* For example, there are many Bible teachers whose emphasis disturbs me but whom I will not oppose, simply because they aren't against Jesus! And because I have generally been favored throughout the Body of Christ with a reputation for biblical balance in my preaching and teaching, I will often be urged to stance myself against others of special emphasis or idiosyncratic style. But at the price of the critics' disapproval, I've committed to leave to the Holy Spirit those whose emphasis or style seems off center to me. And my tolerance is motivated—indeed, *required!*—for this one reason alone: *"He that isn't against us is on our side"!*

The unusual encounter with me that Paul relates in this book occurred some time later; that moment I happened to be kneeling beside him at a prayer meeting. We were hardly acquainted at all at the time, and how he happened to ask me to be his pastor is his story to tell. But it was my decision to make as to whether I would accept his request.

I did so, not because he and Jan would or could attend my congregation (too far away), and not because the elders of our church could be charged with any authority or accountability for their lives or ministry. I simply said, "Yes" because I saw another imperfect servant of Christ like myself, reaching out as though to say, "Sometimes I need somebody to pray with, to correct me, to encourage or assist me in tough decisions—to help me be a better man, a better husband, or a better father." I couldn't say no to an honest heart, humble enough to admit its finiteness, although the man was obviously gifted, capable, and anointed (and eventually renowned).

So in the limited sense I have described, I became Paul and Jan's pastor. And on at least a dozen occasions over the past nearly three decades, Anna and I have sat with them, helping them deal with tough times, praying with them over hard decisions, or responding to them as shepherds when comfort was needed. I've been confrontational with Paul on a few occasions, too, and I admire any Christian leader who will invite someone to speak with him when he knows that person may challenge what he's doing.

Which is why Paul asked me to read this book.

"Pastor," he said, "because I'm mentioning a number of the hard things that have taken place, naming people, and expressing my feelings, I want to ask you to examine what I've written to see if you think I'm being unkind or unchristian in any way."

"Paul," I first responded, "I'll be glad to critique the manuscript. But may I begin by saying first: You need to send any portion of the book where you mention a key person to *that* person for their examination. I'm not saying you need to let them rewrite your book, but you do need to let them know what you're saying and at least allow their feedback."

He hesitated only a moment, then, "You're right—that *is* the right thing to do. I'll set that in motion immediately." And it's *that* willingness to seek to do the right thing that I appreciate in Paul Crouch. I don't know a stronger man than this tough-hided, German-temperamented, business-minded Christian leader. But neither do I know of any brother in Christ less ready to insist on his own righteousness or more ready to accept refocusing or correction at crucial points. And I don't know a man more committed or more consumed with reaching his generation with the Gospel of God's love in Jesus Christ.

As I was reading these pages you're about to enter, I winced a few times at what has been related of storm, stress, and strain between people. But I was also pleased to discover reconciliation and redemption occurring between parties who earlier had wrestled with human failure, temper, blindness, or self-serving tactics. Not every dispute referenced here has been fully settled, but in every case I believe the writing of this book will assist toward the refining of relationships and the strengthening of the whole Body of Christ.

Paul and Jan Crouch have been raised up by God to do a most unique work in this generation, and it inevitably requires a most unique pair of personalities to accomplish that work. I'm grateful for their obedience to their call and for their persistence in pursuing it. But most of all, I'm grateful for their willingness to keep growing in Jesus—to keep "the heart of a child" so the Holy Spirit may not only speak to them and use them dramatically, but to also allow Him to teach and correct them as a son and daughter of our Heavenly Father.

So, let me introduce you to Paul—our brother, and to this book—his testimony. I said at the beginning, "This is a volatile book." So, now, let me interpret *how* it is explosive and combustible in its potential. It can, if you'll let it, *explode* preconceptions and smallness of soul, as God did in me those years ago. It can also *ignite* a flame of new love in your heart for Christ, His Church, and His servants as you share the story of one man's growth in grace.

Paul originally wrote it to his two sons, but he has rewritten and expanded this volume to *every* son and daughter of the Most High, who I know will both enjoy and profit from reading. And I think you'll find it far more than the beautiful testimony it is: you'll find it a teaching instrument drawing you, as it has drawn me, closer to the heart of God—the Father of us all.

One of Christ's shepherds,
Jack W. Hayford, Pastor
The Church On The Way
Van Nuys, California

SPECIAL INTRODUCTION
TO MY TWO SONS

TO MY DEAR SONS, PAUL JR. AND MATTHEW, I WRITE this account of the calling of God and the miraculous birth of what has become the TRINITY BROADCASTING NETWORK, with mixed and at times tormented emotions. For several years I have wrestled with the concept of this account as to how it should be presented and even *IF* it should be recorded. In your early teens you were both a vital part of TBN's birth and development— indeed it was your comfort, love, support, and yes, even your humor that kept your mother and me from checking into the psychiatric ward of *"Happy Acres"* at times! But of course, most of the behind-the-scenes struggles, battles, conflicts, and at times despair we spared you from because of your tender years.

I can tell you, now that you are both spiritually and physically strong young men with families of your own, the FULL story of how God brought us through the deep waters, the fiery furnaces, the lions' dens, even what seemed to be the pits of hell itself to establish perhaps the greatest voice for God in the history of the world. I'm sure some will take issue with this statement, but I speak not only in the spiritual sense, but also with the knowledge that this great voice is able to access multiplied billions simultaneously around the world! This is, indeed, the first generation that has even had the technology to accomplish this.

By the way, I could not be more proud of you both—to see God's hand and calling on you—now working in your own ministries, as well as TBN, and still contributing in so many ways to the continued growth and expansion of the network. A couple of "chips off the old block," say what? I guess dads do like to take a little credit for their sons' success, but it seems I hear your mother's sweet voice somewhere in the background, too!

So, why am I writing this detailed account of the miraculous birth and development of TBN to you? Most of all to encourage you and to tell you of a God that is more than able—abundantly able—to bring you through every fiery trial MORE THAN A CONQUEROR through Jesus Christ! Also, to warn you of some pitfalls, dangers, disappointments, and traps of the evil one that await you, too, up the road!

I suppose the hardest lesson your mother and I had to learn in all of our experiences was the tragic fact that much of our hurt, pain, discouragement, and disappointments came from—I think you already know—our brothers and sisters in Christ! Oh, the world has hurled many a missile, too—you expect it from them—

but when it comes from those you love the most, well, the pain is indescribable. I have taken much comfort from the story of Joseph and his brothers. When their father, Jacob, favored his one son with a "coat of many colors"—you know the story well! The jealous rage that followed is one of the most tragic and yet one of the most triumphant stories in the Bible.

Well, Christian television has surely been our modern-day "coat of many colors"! Why God chose to call your mother and me into this highly specialized ministry is a mystery known only to Him. There have been times when this coat has felt more like a curse than a blessing. I have cried out to God on more than one occasion to take it back—to let this cup pass—but then the cloud would lift, the "Red Sea" would open, the morning would dawn. To our wonder and amazement another great station would sign on the air!

Satellites were launched! Holy Beamers rolled off the assembly line! Cable stations, fiber optics, and the vast Internet were born. Foreign nations began to open up—a night when I would throw a thousand salvation slips into the air in ecstasy as partners rejoiced from coast to coast! *Ah, the memories—the miracles that only God could have brought to pass.*

Surely "God hath chosen the foolish things to confound the wise." Surely God wanted the world to see that TBN was HIS miracle so that *"no flesh should glory in his presence" (1 Corinthians 1:27, 29).*

You are probably already aware that some very well-known names of Christian leaders will fill the pages of this account. Names like Jim and Tammy Bakker, Ralph Wilkerson, Pat Boone, Demos Shakarian, Thomas Zimmerman, and John Wesley

Fletcher will have some roles in this drama. Many not so well-known names like Ward Vanguard, Paul and Joyce Toberty, Merv Mattlock, Heath Kaiser, Jerry Rose, Richard Bott, Ray Wilson, plus many others will play out major and minor roles in this drama. Out of respect to the sensitive nature of certain issues related in this book, some individual's names have been changed. So I warn you now: some of the scenes will be sad—some will be ugly—some will even be downright funny—but some will also be victorious beyond compare!

The good news that I can share with you after thirty years of indescribable battle is this: *Just as Joseph and his brothers were finally reunited and reconciled as a family in love, your mother and I have come to know the great joy of total and unconditional forgiveness, the blessings of restored fellowship with those who had hurt us most, and the overwhelming success of a ministry that finally gets into line with the plan and purpose of God.*

Finally, it is the story of God's great big beautiful family—yes, all of my sons and daughters within the Body of Christ! They really are the greatest, you know. They have loved us, prayed for us, and supported us even when the TV screen was snowy and the set was a Sears shower curtain with two folding chairs! They have laughed and cried with us as we rode this giant roller coaster together—at the top when our breath was gone, seeing the glorious and dizzying heights of this world. We have screamed with delight and sometimes terror as we plunged down through another valley of testing and despair.

Yes, thirty years ago, with one borrowed camera, a shower curtain, and only two hours a night on a station we did not even own, our wonderful partners helped us name it *THE TRINITY BROADCASTING NETWORK.* The world laughed—many in the church world laughed—but with more than 4,000 stations and twenty-six satellites on the air worldwide, well, they're not laughing anymore.

So my sons, fasten your spiritual seat belts. Our journey begins—the good, the bad, and the ugly, but also the glories of a mighty voice that now girdles the globe! *All aboard!*

Sincerely,
Dad

I am recording this so that future generations will also praise the Lord for all that He has done. And a people that shall be created shall praise the Lord. (Psalm 102:18 TLB)

CHAPTER ONE

I HAD NO FATHER—BUT GOD!

And I heard a voice from heaven, saying . . . Write, Blessed are the dead which die in the Lord . . . that they may rest from their labours; and their works do follow them. (Revelation 14:13)

I HAD JUST TURNED SEVEN WHEN MOTHER AWOKE me. Sitting on the edge of my bed, crying softly, she said, "Daddy left us last night . . . he is . . ." Her voice broke as she tried valiantly to hold back the tears. "He is with Jesus now." The date was June 1, 1941.

My father, Andrew Crouch, had been a hell-raiser in his youth. As a rebellious teenager he had been literally horsewhipped by his father. (My sons got off pretty easy after all, didn't they?) Hurt and angry, he had run away from home vowing to be—*ready for this?*—a professional gambler!

But Grandma—ah, my dear Grandma Crouch—you could never run from her prayers! Grandma was actually the preacher, and Grandpa, the farmer. She packed a big tent on the rumble seat of her Model-T Ford and preached Pentecost from Texas to the Canadian border in the 1890s and on into the early 20th century.

What a lady, this woman of God! She had come from a Mennonite background of German stock. I never remember her in anything but her long black dress with the white starched collar and wrist cuffs. She was the matriarch of the Crouch family. Anyone with a problem went to see Agnes Leaming Crouch. She always seemed to have the answer or at least could pray you through to it!

Her eyes were transparent blue and it seemed she could peer into the very depths of your soul! You never lied to Grandma—forget it—she could read your mind. *Those eyes . . . those eyes!* Even a financial problem was no match for Grandma. She could disappear into the bathroom and always turn up a five or a ten. I always wondered—*where on her person did she stash it?*

This is not my biography, but I need to tell you a story about one Saturday afternoon I will never forget. The rest of the family had gone shopping and Grandma and I were left alone. I was about eighteen, heading for Bible college in the fall. She said, "Son, God is calling you into the ministry"—you really didn't have a choice; if God hadn't called you, Grandma prayed you into it! "I want to tell you some of the many wonderful miracles the Lord has done for me," she continued. I will never forget that afternoon as story after story poured from this saint of God who, it seemed, was already living most of the time in another world. She came back only occasionally to tend to earthly matters! I will always know that most of the blessings our family enjoys are a result of the life of this saintly woman who, like Abraham, left all to follow God.

The story I remember most vividly was the day Grandpa Frank and their three sons, Andrew, James, and John, went to town to buy their first Model-T Ford. (My dad was Andrew. All children and grandchildren had to have Bible names.) Grandpa Frank had never driven anything but teams of horses, but in those days the car salesman gave you a twenty-minute driving course and turned you loose with the infernal machine! Returning home, Grandpa lost control of the car while crossing the Grand Fork bridge and plunged into the riverbed below.

Grandma's eyes filled with tears as she continued her story. "God spoke to me, honey," she said. "He spoke out loud—I was carrying an armload of firewood in to the cookstove when God spoke," again she emphasized, "out loud!

"God said, 'Frank and the boys have gone over the bridge—they are in the riverbed—you must hitch up the team and go get them!'" Her crystal-blue eyes glistened as she relived the traumatic moment. "I threw the wood into the air and immediately obeyed the voice of the Lord! Sure enough, just as God had spoken, there they were, Frank and the boys—all unconscious, all with broken bones! I loaded them on the wagon," she continued, "and headed home."

By now the neighbors had caught sight of the tragedy and had summoned the doctor. But Grandma didn't believe in doctors. She actually refused to let the doctor see them and instead anointed them with oil and prayed the prayer of faith! Her angel face was aglow with joy as she said, "God healed them, honey! He healed them that day—they got up that evening and did their chores!" For years, the old-timers around Woodward, Iowa, told and retold the miraculous story of the day God healed Frank

Crouch and his boys Andrew, James, and John—broken bones and all!

Years later my father, in his rebellion, tried to run from his mother's prayers, but his professional gambling career was cut short in a smoke-filled pool hall playing poker in a little South Dakota town. As he looked up . . . *across the table sat the Devil himself!* Terrified, he saddled his horse and rode like a man possessed back to the home place in Iowa. There at his mother's knee he surrendered to Jesus and was later called into the ministry.

In 1912 my dad and mother joined Grandma Agnes and Grandpa Frank, Uncle John and Aunt Dora, in a missionary expedition to the land of Egypt. God had spoken to Grandma and Grandpa to sell the Iowa farm to finance this first missions thrust into Egypt in the 20th century.

The stories are both thrilling and tragic. Travel was a nightmare. First of all, it took six weeks by ocean liner just to get from New York to Cairo, Egypt! The trains were antique, open-window railway cars that often passed through choking sandstorms in 100-plus-degree temperatures. Auto breakdowns were serious problems with repair parts three months away in the United States!

It is interesting to note here that my father never rode in an airplane, never even saw a television set, and satellites had not been conceived in the mind of man! Surely we are that generation that the prophet Daniel spoke of when he wrote:

> *But thou, O Daniel . . . seal the book, even to the time of the end: many shall run to and fro, and knowledge shall be increased. (Daniel 12:4)*

Cousin Rachel contracted smallpox and died. Her grave in Egypt is a stark reminder of the price paid by those early pioneers. On the other hand, there were glorious victories—churches raised up that remain to this day as trophies of God's grace. Mother told me stories of the power of God falling in those early meetings. One of the great signs and wonders was the glorious baptism of the Holy Spirit upon simple peasant people. She told of how they would often speak in perfect English by the power of the Holy Spirit, praising and magnifying God!

Some years later, in 1936, after we children were born, our own family returned to Egypt, but it was then that Dad's health broke. I was only four at the time, but I remember one hair-raising night! Seniah, our nurse who had come to help with Dad, slept just around the corner from my bed. Suddenly, in the middle of the night, she screamed! Rushing to the bathroom, she grabbed Dad's old-fashioned razor and began slashing her arm! When we finally restrained her, the marks of a deadly scorpion bite were clearly seen. She knew that the wound must be bled to rid her arm of the venom! How strange the memories that are etched in the recesses of our minds.

Needless to say, that night left its mark upon us all, but especially on Dad's weakened heart. The doctor finally advised us that Dad should return to the United States immediately. So I said good-bye to my little Egyptian friends and the only life or home that I could remember.

On the way home I contracted the most deadly form of bacillary dysentery. Our ocean liner was forced to make an unscheduled stop in Genoa, Italy, where I was rushed by ambulance to the hospital. For thirty days I hovered between life and death. A special serum was ordered from Switzerland; but now World War II was raging. Hitler and Mussolini had joined in an Axis alliance—we were now in enemy territory!

The doctor told Mother that the crisis would come—the fever would peak and the prognosis was not good. Mother would tell me years later how she saw the shadowy form of the death angel enter my hospital room that night. She recounted how she had literally stretched her body across my bed, pleading the blood of Jesus and refusing to let the death angel come near!

The crisis passed and I began to slowly recover. But now, full-scale war had broken out—foreigners, especially Americans, were ordered to leave. *We were the enemy!* In my weakened condition they allowed a little German nurse, Heidi Hanover, to accompany our family home to Missouri.

How unsearchable the strategy of God. While in America, Heidi received Jesus before returning to her native Germany. After the war ended in 1945 she wrote and recounted that all during Hitler's rampage she had conducted underground prayer meetings and church services and had led many to Christ!

Dad tried to resume his pastoral duties in our hometown of St. Joseph, Missouri, but a stroke one fateful night was final. My precious pioneer father had "ceased from his labors." For many weeks before his home going he would tell all visitors before they left— "IN JUNE I WILL BE WELL!" Indeed he was WELL as he entered his eternal reward in the early morning of June 1.

Nellie Pumphrey, classic soprano from Dad's St. Joseph pastorate, sang a most beautiful and touching tribute at his home-going celebration: "The Song of the Sower."

"Over and over, yes deeper and deeper
My heart is pierced through with earth's
Sorrowing cry.
But the tears of the sower and
the song of the reaper,
will mingle together in joy
by and by."

As we said good-bye to Dad that day, the realization seized me, at seven years of age, that I would never see him again in this life. Now I really had no father . . . but God.

CHAPTER TWO

HELLO WORLD!

LIFE ISN'T EASY AT BEST, BUT WITHOUT A FATHER—
well, a boy's life is tough. I'm glad my sons didn't have to bear that
cross, although I know those years that TBN was coming to birth
were hard for us all. I'm sure there were days that my sons felt they
did not have a father either! We'll talk about those days later in
this writing, and maybe we will all understand better why Jan and
I were not always there when they needed us.

Many wonderful souls reached out to Mother, my sister Ruth,
and me during those difficult days following Dad's death. My
older sister, Naomi, was grown and married; my older brothers,
Philip and John, were also grown. Philip and his wife, Hazel, had
remained as missionaries in Egypt, and John had just gotten married and moved on into business.

The older children helped Mother a lot. I remember Philip and Hazel would send some support even from their meager missionary allotment. John paid our rent for several years—it was twenty dollars a month. Mother was a seamstress and she worked long hours making the blue uniforms that all the girls wore at Central Bible Institute, which was located a block from our little cottage.

Every Christmas and Thanksgiving we could count on a delicious turkey, hand delivered by Brother E. S. Williams, who was the general superintendent of the Assemblies of God. What an example of Jesus this man and his wife were. He was later my theology professor when I attended Central Bible Institute. I will never forget his kindness. His example as a Christian left an indelible mark on me.

The true Body of Christ is really wonderful! They never make the news stories but, believe me, they are there—Jesus' true Body is alive and well and has been in every generation.

The years passed quickly and when I was about twelve years of age, one such saint of God was destined to not only make a mark upon my life, but would change the direction of it forever. Hazel Bakewell was a piano teacher and also a member of our church, Central Assembly of God in Springfield, Missouri. Hazel, knowing of our financial situation, called Mother one day and offered to give me free piano lessons! I think Mother secretly hoped that I would become a great musical virtuoso, so she urged me to accept Sister Bakewell's generosity.

I went, but soon learned to hate every lesson. Practice was a bore, the bus ride each week took me away from baseball, and let's face it—I just didn't have *piano chips* in the right hemisphere. But after a few weeks Mother took courage. I would ask to leave early for my lesson and would return sometimes hours late. She hoped that I had finally learned to love the piano. But when Mother checked up on me, Hazel made it clear it was not the piano that had kept me. Instead it was her husband, Lawrence, who had this mess of wires and tubes called a "HAM RIG" in the basement!

I spent hundreds of hours with Lawrence calling, *"CQ, CQ, this is WØCGJ calling CQ—over."* We would turn off the transmitter and wait. Suddenly through the static would come a reply!

"WØCGJ, this is W6XYZ returning your call!"

Amateur radio became my obsession, and at fifteen years of age I passed the FCC test and became a licensed "ham." I finally scraped up enough spare parts and after many blown fuses, one which darkened much of north Springfield, WØAVQ came on the air from 505 West Evergreen Street in Springfield, Missouri!

The technology was primitive by today's standards: coils of wire wound on oatmeal boxes, tubes, transformers, resistors, and condensers—most everything was hand wired, but it worked! I loved the 10 meter band because we could talk to people in Europe, Africa, even Asia and Australia. I loved to watch the meters kick as you talked—also the deep blue glow of the high-voltage rectifier tubes—they would flicker bright and dim with the modulation of your voice.

I remember so clearly one night as the awesome thought hit me—*My voice is literally leaping off that antenna wire into thin air and this guy in Japan can hear me!* I wrote an essay for my high school civics class in which I said I would one day use this invention of shortwave radio to send the Gospel around the world. Little did I dream that our weak "ham gear" would one day become Superpower KTBN, a two-and-a-half-million-watt short-wave radio station that today is literally sending the Gospel to virtually every spot on earth from its location in Salt Lake City, Utah.

Nor did I dream at this time that those electromagnetic beams would someday carry a full-color picture to the homes of America and the world. We will talk about TV in later chapters, but I will say here that I was sixteen years old when I saw my first TV set. I will never forget standing with my "ham buddies," noses pressed against the glass of Harry Reed Radio & Supply on Boonville Street in Springfield, Missouri, watching a snowy test pattern from a TV station in Kansas City nearly 200 miles away!

Surely God ordains our lives and callings, and I will ever know that He ordained this powerful media of radio and TV to proclaim His Gospel in these last days. I will always be grateful to so many who helped me and guided me during these early formative years of what would become TBN! Surely the Bakewells, who put up with me through those early years, will share in the reward for the millions of souls brought into the Kingdom through TBN! Hazel forgave me for not learning piano and lived to see the great miracle of TBN. Lawrence also went home to be with Jesus. He, too, lived to see in part God's great plan for using those amazing electromagnetic waves to "Give the winds a MIGHTY VOICE—*Jesus saves! Jesus saves!*"

After graduating from high school in 1952, I entered Central Bible Institute rather than the FBI academy (which is what I wanted). I knew down deep, however, I was making the right decision. I immediately formed an amateur radio "Ham Club," and with a directional beam antenna on top of the water tower we continued to talk and witness to many other "hams" and short-wave listeners. We also contacted other stations of missionaries on foreign fields and relayed messages on occasion to the foreign missions department of the Assemblies of God; but just how radio and Bible school would all come together was still not clear.

But then I chanced upon the magazine article that said: "COVER YOUR CAMPUS WITH CARRIER CURRENT RADIO." *What was this? A new kind of radio station—no license necessary? Send the radio waves through the electrical wires and the FCC doesn't care?* Best of all, you can tune it in on a plain old radio set and the listener won't even know the difference.

For days we scrounged up tubes, condensers, resistors—fifty whole watts of power! And after a few more blown fuses, the thing WORKED! KCBI was born! Word spread through the dormitories: *Official sign-on TONIGHT!* With all the pomp and circumstance, drama, fanfare, and ceremony of NBC, our national anthem crackled through the wires, and finally those first historic words: *"HELLO WORLD!"* Not as scientifically momentous as Samuel F. B. Morse's "What hath God wrought?" or Alexander Graham Bell's "Come in here, Mr. Watson," but spiritually I see these TWO WORDS today as words of profound PROPHETIC significance. God knew fifty years later we would see over 4,000 TV and radio stations linked together by twenty-six satellites—a superpower shortwave radio station, fiber optics, the cyberspace of the Internet, Holy Beamers, and now great translation centers to make the Gospel speak in the languages of the nations. Indeed—*"WHAT HATH GOD WROUGHT?"!*

But the lesson I want everyone to learn here is that God has an exciting destiny for the life of every child of God, just as there has been for mine. Watch for the little things as well as the big. I am sure it was no accident that I was born in 1934, the same year Congress established the Federal Communications Commission. I've had a love affair with the FCC for more than fifty years! I wonder if they feel the same?

To my sons, Paul Jr. and Matt, I can see that God's destiny for your lives is already becoming clear as you both continue to grow in the many skills and technology of television and other media. You both have already come through some fiery trails of your own, and I rejoice to see the hand of God at work in your lives. I wish I could tell everyone that it gets easier as you move on toward the *"prize of the high calling of God"*—but it does not. No, it won't be easy, but I am a witness that our God is able and will bring us all through every fiery furnace, *"more than a conqueror"!* You'll see many examples of this in the next pages of my letter to you.

CHAPTER THREE

OUT OF EGYPT

I TOLD YOU EARLIER THAT THIS IS NOT A BIOGRAPHY of my life, but I do need to tell you a few significant milestones that led to and contributed to the miracle birth of TBN. It is wonderful and amazing to look back on one's life and see clearly why certain things and events happened as they did. At the time some of them seemed devastating—even a complete defeat—but in time it became clear that the Great Master Planner was at work. Here is an important lesson of life: NEVER ACCEPT AN APPARENT DEFEAT AS FINAL. In fact, never accept an apparent defeat as a defeat! To those of us who are called of God, there is NO SUCH THING AS A DEFEAT!

Remember Dad Billheimer? In his book, *Destined for the Throne,* he taught us by godly example that these so-called defeats are simply "New challenges to our faith." As we grow spiritually, God can trust us with bigger problems! "God's hurdles," if you please, "on life's track." Whoever heard of an athlete, training for an obstacle race, pleading with his trainer to remove the obstacles? So, how can we ever be overcomers if there is never anything to overcome?

Dad goes on to say, "Let us show all onlookers that we believe Romans 8:28 and Ephesians 1:11 when 'bad news' is given to us that God is big enough, powerful enough, and loving enough to take care of any apparent defeat in a way that will bring even more glory to His Name when we have overcome!"

I wish I had known this back in 1955 when I graduated from Bible college! Like most of my class, I was ready to take on the WORLD! *Satan—watch it! PFC is on the warpath! HELLO WORLD!*

❧

I was just this high when the call came for me to go to Egypt! My brother Philip was due for furlough. He and his wife Hazel had stayed on when our family left nearly twenty years earlier. All through World War II and up through the mid-fifties, they had faithfully served with a missionary legend—Miss Lillian Trasher, also known as the "Nile Mother." Miss Lillian was a lot like Grandmother Crouch. She was a real pioneer who had gone to Egypt around the turn of the century with no support, no backing of any denomination or missions board—strictly on faith! They don't make many like Lillian Trasher or Agnes Crouch anymore!

Miss Lillian had founded an orphanage in the early 1900s that had held more than 2,000 boys and girls. The stories of God's provision, especially during the critical World War II years, would fill a book of its own. Some of those stories I was privileged to hear directly from Miss Lillian on her first furlough visit back to the U.S. after more than forty years of service to the children of Egypt. This rare visit coincided with my graduation from Bible college. Two brief stories that I will never forget left an indelible mark on my memory and have both encouraged and blessed me through the years.

During the war, anarchy and looting were common even in the southern Egyptian city of Assiut. The soldiers of fortune who had pillaged and looted the city now turned their greed toward the orphanage just across the Nile River. To even think of taking from helpless orphans is a testament to the depravity of human nature without God. The lead scout had scaled the protective wall to spy out the compound when suddenly, from across the Nile, a shot pierced the stillness. The thief fell dead—pierced through the heart by a stray bullet! Needless to say, his cohorts fled into the darkness—Miss Lillian and 2,000 children were spared by the hand of God.

Miss Trasher told me of numerous times that the children would file into the dining room with not a crust of bread to feed them, but with tears in her saintly eyes she said, "Son, we never left the dining room hungry!" A truck would pull up—a wagonload would arrive—always a knock on the door even as little heads were bowed to say grace over empty plates.

One such amazing story occurred during the height of the war as General Rommel of the Nazi Third Reich engaged the British and American forces across North Africa. Only a miracle of God kept the German army from taking Cairo, which would have given Egypt to Hitler. As the war raged, a German supply ship was captured by the British. The commander knew of Miss Lillian's home and need. A call came over the antique phone one day (a minor miracle in itself) and the general asked if the children could use a boatload of food supplies! Needless to say, a convoy of trucks laden with staples that would see them through most of the war rolled up the Nile valley to Miss Lillian and her children. I'm sure Hitler never knew it, but God used even a madman to feed His little ones in need! Don't ever doubt Him, my children.

> *I have been young, and now I am old; yet have I not seen the righteous forsaken nor his seed begging bread. (Psalm 37:25)*

Well, since Philip and Hazel were coming home on furlough, Miss Lillian asked me to return to Egypt with her to help look after 2,000 precious Egyptian orphans. I was elated! Surely this was God—Grandma Crouch, then Mom and Dad, Phil and Hazel, and now me, a missionary to Egypt!

I itinerated the summer months of 1955, raising my monthly support. Late in the fall, with barrels and trunks packed and waiting in New York, the cablegram arrived the very day I was to board the train: *"President Nassar nationalizes the Suez Canal . . . STOP . . . Nation in crisis . . . STOP . . . All foreign visas cancelled . . . STOP . . . Please pray."*

My whole world collapsed. Later, Miss Lillian wrote to Mother, "Perhaps this was your Abraham-Isaac test. He saw you were willing to send your son to a dark and heathen land. God has some better plan for Paul. Tell him Mother Lillian sends her love."

Remember, there is no such thing as defeat for the child of God. Remember, we never accept even an apparent defeat as final. Little did I realize that this strange turn of events would lead me down an entirely new and different road; one that would give meaning and substance to my fifty-watt *"Hello World"* radio station. Nor did I know that this road would lead through an old sawdust-floor camp meeting tabernacle where I would meet a stunning Southern belle who would one day be . . . well, let's move on—it really gets exciting now!

CHAPTER FOUR

ON TO SOUTH DAKOTA!

SO NOW WHAT TO DO? MY HOPES AND VISION SO high—dashed. I had visited many churches, told all my friends, was on my way—after all, Egypt was in Africa and there was a certain mystique, even romance, in being a missionary to Africa! I may have even imagined myself another David Livingstone. *Ah, youth, what a blessing and what a burden.* Who said what a shame it is to "waste" youth on young people? I think it was George Bernard Shaw.

Anyway, Brother Noel Perkin, head of the Assemblies of God Foreign Missions Department, had mercy on me and gave me the job of renting the 16mm missions' film library to the churches. It was totally boring. You had to check each print for breaks and torn sprockets, splice it back together, then send it out to another church for a missionary service. One of the films was *Nile Mother*, the story of Miss Lillian's orphanage. Every time I saw the title it was depressing.

In the spring of 1956 things got a little more exciting. A series of mission conventions was conducted from New York to California! At least I would get to see some of the world. I was responsible for the big arc light projector and showed the motion pictures in the large auditoriums. It was fun but also grueling work. Lugging heavy equipment, driving through the night to another city, junk food, little or no sleep, and by summer at the end of the tour I was physically as well as emotionally exhausted. I had had a serious bout with rheumatic fever my first year of Bible school and had lost a whole semester. For thirty days I was ordered to bed by my doctor. Even then he warned me that my heart had been involved and that I would never be able to do heavy manual labor.

One night it struck. I had just retired for the night when, without warning, my heart began to race. After 150 beats a minute I began to black out. I stumbled into Mother's bedroom and collapsed at the foot of the bed. She summoned Dr. Coffelt, who actually came to our cottage in the middle of the night. (Try to get your doctor to do that today!) By the time he arrived I was returning to normal, and after a thorough examination Dr. Coffelt was perplexed—he could find nothing wrong and guessed that I had hyperventilated. He prescribed some sleeping powder and told me to rest for a few days.

By now my missionary disappointment, followed by a job I knew was not for me, had caused me to lapse into a deep melancholy that I could not seem to get on top of. And now a real fear had set in as I wondered when the next heart episode would occur.

Again, Brother Noel Perkin took pity on me and gave me a month's sick leave at half pay. By the way, my pay—full pay—was fifty dollars a week. Of course this was 1956.

Here is where things get exciting! My oldest sister, Naomi, and her husband, Bernard Ridings, pastored the First Assembly of God Church in Rapid City, South Dakota. I had gone to Rapid City most every summer even during high school. Lots of construction work was available in this Air Force base town and you could make $100 a week building houses!

Naomi encouraged Mother and me to come to Rapid City for the month of July because the annual state camp meeting would soon be under way. A well-known camp meeting speaker and Bible teacher, Reverend Edgar Bethany, was scheduled to preach the main evening services. Pastor Bethany was beloved throughout the Assemblies of God, having founded one of the denomination's primary Bible colleges, Southeastern Bible Institute in Lakeland, Florida. Now he was pastoring the leading Assembly of the southeast in Columbus, Georgia, as well as serving as executive presbyter for all of the southeastern states.

Papa Bethany really deserves a chapter all his own. God had saved him as a tough young gang leader in Mobile, Alabama, who had come to break up an old-fashioned tent revival conducted by another turn-of-the-century evangelist, D. P. Holloway. Instead of cutting the ropes and collapsing the tent on the worshippers, as he and his gang had meant to do, conviction seized him and he surrendered his life to Jesus that night. His Jewish father literally threw him out of the home, so he joined D. P. Holloway's team and was later called into the ministry.

Papa Bethany, as all the family called him, was the patriarch of his side of the family—the counterpart to Grandma Agnes Crouch on my side. And what a precious man of God he was. His gentle spirit had been shaped by the worst kind of tragedy in his early years and first marriage. Mattie Herring was his first love and had given him the desire of every man's life—a son. Sadly, the child lived only a few weeks. A second son met a similar fate. In those days the Rh-negative blood disorder was unknown—today a simple blood transfusion remedies the problem. When a third son was born, he lived only a few hours and Papa Bethany had the tortured task of bearing the sad news to his beloved Mattie for the third time. This time she asked to be alone, saying something like, "They need me, Edgar." In minutes, Mattie had joined her three sons in heaven. Papa Bethany buried his beloved wife with their third son resting peacefully in his mother's arms.

Papa Bethany cried out to God for over a year that he might die and join his loved ones in heaven. But God had a better plan for his life. For out of that crushing experience came the sweetest, most gentle spirit I have ever seen in a human being.

In time he returned to the ministry and met a beautiful little nurse, Laurie Elizabeth Leard. He actually led her to Christ in his revival meeting, married her, and this time fathered three beautiful girls—Laurie, Dorothy, and Janice. But I'm getting ahead of my story.

❦

I shall never forget that hot summer day in the old wooden tabernacle in Rapid City. The smell of fresh sawdust sweetened the air, but nothing compared to the sweetness that walked down the aisle—heads turned (especially the boys') as a slight, ninety-eight-pound angel seemed more to glide than walk toward the front of the room. Head down—timid it seemed to me—yet the bright red dress contrasted with the retiring, even shy, demeanor of this stunning young lady!

She can't be from these parts, or I would have seen her before, I thought. *She can't even be a South Dakota girl.* My thoughts were racing now! *Could it be the camp meeting speaker's daughter? No way . . . she's too . . . well, just too . . . that dress . . . but who?*

But as I watched, transfixed, she headed straight for the left front of the tabernacle, up where the district officials and dignitaries sat. I have to confess I did not get too much out of the service that night. I'm afraid I watched the dignitary section more than I did the pulpit.

At the conclusion of the service, after a very short altar session, I moseyed over to politely meet and welcome the esteemed speaker's wife, Sister Edgar Bethany. My real purpose was wonderfully answered as Sister Bethany not only thanked me for my warm welcome to Rapid City, but—*hallelujah*—also introduced me to—sure enough—her stunning daughter, *Janice Wendell Bethany!*

After a bit of small talk I learned, to my delight, that she was coming that fall to my hometown of Springfield, Missouri, to attend Evangel College, the Assemblies of God liberal arts school! *Bingo!* This was it—my lucky year! But then the bad news—she was going very steady with a young man in her hometown of Columbus, Georgia! Oh, well, maybe Egypt would finally open up or, worse yet, maybe I was destined to clean and repair 16mm missions films for the churches. My depression deepened as I said good night and something like, "Hope to see you in Springfield sometime."

I did not know it till much later, but I had made a pretty fair impression on prissy Miss Bethany that night myself. I learned later, after having told her my whole Egypt story, that she had remarked to her mother, "What would you think of my being a missionary to Egypt?" I'm not sure to this day what her mother's response was!

Well, summer camp meeting ended, and after a month of rest and spiritual refreshing, it was back to Springfield, and yes—the film department. I dreamed often of that haunting little red dress that belled out at the bottom, gliding down the sawdust trail, but did not have the courage to even call over to the college to see if Miss Bethany had actually made it to Springfield. After all, she was going steady—*rats!*

Finally, to my great surprise, I bumped head-on into my little "Scarlett" Southern belle going out the back door of my home church, Central Assembly of God—yes, the headquarter church of our denomination. This time she was arm in arm with Bud Zimmerman, son of the General Superintendent of the whole Assemblies of God! Well, that did it! The last glimmer of hope was snuffed out. After an awkward hello and a few mumbled amenities, I headed for home all the more tormented by this answer to any boy's dream, which now I knew was beyond my class or reach.

After all, Jan's dad was one of the top officials of the church and I was just the lowly film jockey at the Foreign Missions Department and now . . . *Bud Zimmerman!* Oh, there were plenty of other girls. Ruthie Syvelle, the switchboard operator, had a crush on me, and I had other dates, *but ah—that dress . . . that red dress!*

Finally it happened. The switchboard gal rang me one afternoon. Ruthie called me quite often for all kinds of silly reasons, but this time I knew something different was up! "You've got a call, Paul," she said rather caustically. "I think it's that Jan Bethany from Georgia."

I'll always know she eavesdropped on the call, but my heart was racing too fast for me to care!

"Hi Paul," came the cheery voice.

"Is this *the* Jan Bethany?" I asked.

"Yes, and I'm calling to see if you might like to attend our Campus Classics night this Friday—I'm, well . . . " she faltered a little. "I'm singing, and I thought you might like to join in the fun!"

Silence reigned for at least thirty seconds. *Is she asking me for a date?* I trembled. "Well, uh, sure," I mumbled. "I can change my plans for Friday," I lied.

Well, folks, that was the first date of many! I managed another the next night and the next and the next. I don't think we missed a single night for the next thirty days or so. By May, at the end of the school year, we were engaged and had even set the date: August 25, 1957.

Don't ever accuse us Germans of being slow!

CHAPTER FIVE

THE SUMMER OF '57

AH, THE SUMMER OF '57—IT WAS INDEED THE longest summer of my life. Each day was an eternity as I waited for our BIG DAY! Even my film cleaning and splicing was a joy! The clouds were fluffier, the birds sang more melodiously—everyone was happy for me—all except Ruthie the switchboard operator. I told everyone of the BIG DATE—even my ham-radio buddies. Folks from Copenhagen to Hong Kong knew I had found the girl of my dreams—I was getting married! (I had long since given up piano, but I still spent time in Mr. Bakewell's basement talking to "hams" around the world. Hazel, my former piano teacher, groused that she hoped my new wife could play the piano—after all, anyone going into the ministry should at least have a wife who played and sang!)

26

I made one trip that July to Columbus, Georgia, in my little Volkswagen Bug just to meet my prospective new in-laws and the rest of Jan's family. I found the legendary Southern hospitality to be absolutely true and met some of the most gracious and loving people of my entire life. I cherish many of those dear people to this very day, though many of them have gone home to be with the Lord.

For several days Jan and I planned and dreamed, addressed wedding invitations, attended her dad's great church, North Highland Assembly of God, where in another thirty days or so we would be married. I could hardly pull myself away, but it was back to Springfield for some final preparations—and of course, my "films" were waiting for me!

At last the great day arrived! Mother and a few of my friends formed a two-car motorcade and we were off to Georgia. My brother-in-law, Bernard Ridings, was to be my best man—*hallelujah—we were almost there!*

🌿

I really do not have to try to describe the emotions of that day to you, Paul and Matt. Both of you have been blessed with beautiful brides just as I was. Paul, your choice of Tawny Dryden, and Matt, your Laurie Orndorff, prove that you have the same good taste as "dear old dad"! I think God gave us this "joy unspeakable and full of glory" experience as a little foretaste of the ultimate wedding of His Bride, the Church, to His Son Jesus. If this earthly experience is only an "earnest of our inheritance," what will THAT DAY be like? Someday soon we will know and even those who have not known the joy of an earthly marriage will know the glorious ecstasy of that ultimate union with our Heavenly Bridegroom—*Praise the Lord!*

I must confess that Sunday afternoon of August 25, 1957, is a little hazy and a bit blurred. Jan's precious Papa Bethany honored us with a classic wedding ceremony. The church was packed—the usual tears—why ladies have to cry at weddings, us Germans will never understand. The organ pealed the familiar "Here Comes the Bride." I think every time that classical piece is played, the next line that some joker made up goes through everyone's mind— "Big, fat, and wide." But children, I can tell you that line did not fit my bride! Call me prejudiced, if you will, but the veiled vision that once again glided down that aisle was the most beautiful, the most stunning, the most gorgeous, the most glorious . . . well, adjectives finally run out.

I'm sure my heart was close to hyperventilation once again—this time for pure joy! We had the usual candles, flower girl, ring bearer, bridesmaids, groomsmen, and vows. Ruthie Syvelle even gave me up and sang the only song I remember, "Whither Thou Goest, I Will Go," a sweet and even haunting melody that still rings in the deepest recesses of my memory. The verse goes on to say:

> *Wherever thou lodgest, I will lodge*
> *Thy people shall be my people, my love*
> *Whither thou goest, I will go.*

The reception was pure agony. I never could stand small talk, punch with ice cream floating on top, or tasteless wedding cake, but finally the bouquet was tossed—by the way, Ruthie caught it, thank God—then came the rice and shoe polish all over my VW Bug with *JUST MARRIED* and we were off! Off for a classic honeymoon in the Great Smoky Mountains of Gatlinburg, Tennessee. Do I really need to say that I do not remember much about Gatlinburg or the Great Smokies? Just read the Song of Solomon or remember your glorious days of aloneness with your new bride! I can tell you one thing for sure, my Jan was a pure bride—a truth I will cherish all my life. Sadly this is a rather rare virtue in these days of so-called sexual liberation.

Finally it was home to Springfield, Missouri, and a little duplex on Hovey Street just a couple of blocks from my beloved film department at the Foreign Missions Department, which was in the same building with the Gospel Publishing House (GPH) of the Assemblies of God. The inside joke at the GPH was to call it "God's Poor House"—partly true since my salary was $50 a week. Let me hasten to say that I was given a generous raise of $5 a week since I would now be supporting a new wife!

As I told you earlier, I knew that the film library was not my ultimate destiny or calling from God. But during those early days of marriage we were too busy setting up housekeeping in our little two-room duplex to worry about it. And besides, we were so in love that a shack on the backside of the moon would have been just fine! Even the film job wasn't so bad with a beautiful new bride to come home to!

But then one day the call came from Bruce, South Dakota, a small farming community in the eastern part of the state with an Assemblies of God church. They needed a new pastor—would we consider coming for a tryout service? Jan and I were both flattered and excited! Maybe, just maybe, this was God's plan for our lives. After all, pastoral psychology had been one of my courses in Bible college. My boss was now Phil Hogan, promotions director for the Foreign Missions Department. He was probably glad to see me go. You did not need to be an Einstein to know that my heart was not in the film rental business.

We arrived in Bruce in the dead of winter. Don't let the "South" of South Dakota give you visions of palm trees! The winters are brutal, and unless you are into ice-skating, there is not a lot of recreation up there. But it would take more than ice or snow to cool our enthusiasm for what seemed to be an open door— God's next assignment for our new life together.

The Sunday morning service seemed to go well. Believe it or not, Jan and I sang a duet in those days! There will surely be an extra reward for precious souls who suffered through our . . . well, I can't even find a word to describe it! You may have noticed that we do not sing on TBN—how blessed you are! I even played a little piano. Sister Bakewell's efforts were not totally in vain, but unless it was in the key of "G" I was lost. And lest I forget, Jan did a pretty fair job on the vibraharp, but it turned out to be too large an instrument to fit into our VW Bug.

About thirty-five wonderful folks turned out to hear this young pastoral candidate and I gave them all I had! I compiled a little of the best from every sermon I had ever preached and finally gave the benediction. I don't know what I would have preached the next Sunday, since I had exhausted most of my pastoral theology outlines from Bible school days!

The little congregation could not have been kinder. They greeted us warmly and even complimented our singing and my preaching! The head deacon told us, as we were leaving, that the church business meeting would be held the very next Wednesday and that they would be voting on us as pastors. There were twelve actual voting members of the church, and they would make the final decision.

Jan and I, of course, had made this journey a matter of heartfelt and sincere prayer. We really did want the perfect will of God for our lives and ministry that was just beginning. Secretly we had placed a "fleece" before the Lord just as Gideon had done in Judges 6:37–38. We had agreed in prayer that if it was God's perfect will for us to take up pastoral duties in Bruce, South Dakota, that the vote that next Wednesday would be 100 percent unanimous.

❦

With that decision settled in our hearts, we drove on west to Rapid City, South Dakota, where my sister Naomi and her husband, Bernard Ridings, pastored the First Assembly of God in that bustling, western frontier city.

Bernard had asked us to consider moving to Rapid City to work with the church there as assistant pastors. The church was thriving. Rapid City was booming ever since the Strategic Air

Command base had been established there. Ellsworth Air Force Base had brought hundreds of airmen and their families to Rapid City. Several servicemen and their families were already attending, and the opportunities for evangelism were enormous. Jan and I were torn—eastern or western South Dakota? At least we would wait for the deacon's call from Bruce—the business meeting was less than a week away.

Wednesday finally came—and the call. Remember: I told you earlier to watch for the little things, the little signs along the way. Even the great prophet Elijah observed that God was not in the great wind, earthquake, or fire, but rather in the "still small voice" (1 Kings 19:12). Often it is the small, almost insignificant things that ultimately determine our destiny.

The deacon said, "Brother Crouch, I have wonderful news— you have been elected pastor of Bruce Assembly of God!"

My heart leaped—Jan was snuggling her ear as close to the phone as possible trying to hear the verdict. "Praise the Lord," I responded. "What was the actual vote?"

"Oh, my brother," the deacon continued, "it was an overwhelming vote, eleven for and only one against—it was a landslide!"

Oddly enough, my heart was actually relieved. Somehow we both had not felt at complete peace about this move even though we knew God had some new assignment for us. For several seconds I sat in silence, trying to frame the right words to my sincere deacon brother. Finally I said, "My brother, I appreciate the confidence you and the wonderful members have placed in Jan and me, but I must tell you that we cannot accept your gracious invitation to be your pastors."

For a moment there was a stunned silence—finally the deacon protested, "But Brother Crouch, this is the largest majority vote we have ever had for a pastor. Surely one vote . . . "

His voice trailed off as I told him of the sacred fleece Jan and I had placed before the Lord. I asked my deacon brother to express our deepest love and appreciation to the saints at Bruce Assembly as we bade each other farewell.

In retrospect, I now know that only one of the twelve voting members had the mind of the Lord in the selection of their new pastor. I have often remarked while telling this story that when I get to heaven I want to look up that dear member and thank him or her for helping us not miss the perfect will of God for our lives. How do I know that? Stay tuned and you will know—by the way, *"stay tuned"* is a clue! But then, you may already know that!

CHAPTER SIX

GO WEST, YOUNG MAN

SO WEST IT WAS FOR JAN AND ME, AND THIS TIME we felt peace in our spirits as we accepted the post of assistant pastors at First Assembly of Rapid City, South Dakota. We learned to love the Black Hills, rich in the history of the so-called Wild West of frontier America. I already knew it well, having spent several summers there working my way through school. Names such as "Wild Bill" Hickok and "Calamity Jane" were legendary. Mt. Rushmore, Deadwood, and the Homestake Gold Mine are names and places well known to anyone who remembers his American history. Custer's Last Stand took place farther east, but the Badlands and Wall Drugstore are the gateway to this fabled land of fast-flowing trout streams and sweet-smelling ponderosa pines.

While the church welcomed us warmly, the budget could not provide a full living salary, so I had to seek extra employment for living expenses. As God would have it, the first available job turned out to be—*you guessed it*—radio announcer at 250-watt KRSD-AM 1340 on the dial. I had chatted for hours on end on shortwave "ham" radio, but never dreamed of doing a real disc-jockey radio show on a duly FCC-licensed commercial radio station!

Eli Daniels, a U.S. Navy veteran, was the owner. You've heard the expression, "He could cuss like a sailor"? Well, I think the phrase was invented to describe Eli! I must say, however, that Eli respected my faith, and the fact that I was a pastor caused him to often bite his tongue in my presence. You could always tell, however, when Eli had passed through—noses were buried in feverish work and the air was definitely blue!

The program director gave me a half-hour orientation session on how to be an announcer and disc jockey. "Just play the record and tell the folks the name of the tune and who sang it!" With that he walked out of the soundproof door and guess what? In thirty minutes I had graduated from amateur to commercial radio announcer!

I will be eternally grateful that no recordings were made of those first days of my new career, but before long names like Jim Reeves, Hank Locklin, the Everly Brothers, Johnny Cash, Hank Snow, and Earnest Tubb became very familiar to me. Country music was much different back then. Most of it was about life, love, and broken dreams: "I Can't Stop Loving You," "All I Have to Do Is Dream," "Send Me the Pillow That You Dream On." And yes, there was Elvis with "Blue Suede Shoes" and "You Ain't

Nothin' But a Hound Dog." These and countless others became my "tent-making" as Jan and I directed the choir, printed the church bulletins, directed the song service, taught Sunday School, and even did a bit of midweek preaching.

❦

But then an exciting new phase at KRSD radio exploded! Eli received an FCC permit to build KRSD-TV Channel 7, NBC affiliate for Rapid City! Wow—you could cut the excitement with a knife! All of us pitched in—we pulled wires, hung lights, wired TV gear in racks, hooked up cameras and, would you believe, *16mm projectors! Shades of Springfield and the Foreign Missions Film Department.* At least I knew how to thread a film projector, which, as simple as this sounds, turned out to be a valuable and necessary skill!

Looking back I see so very clearly the hand of God as He put me through basic training, yes, boot camp, if you please, for the day HIS network would be born. We'll move on into that in future chapters, but God saw to it that I would be involved in virtually every phase of building a new TV station from the ground up. By today's standards everything was extremely primitive. Black and white, no videotape, everything was either live or on 16mm film. Even the NBC network shows were crude kinescope recordings that were made by filming a TV screen with a 16mm camera and sending prints to all the affiliated network stations.

I pulled the night shift and my favorite was *Wagon Train* with Ward Bond and Robert Horton. If you were into soap operas it was *Young Dr. Malone,* and for live programs, I directed *Romper Room* and the Saturday *Dance Party.* Some of the deacons at First Assembly got a little heartburn on that one, so I had to keep my name off the credits!

I will never forget our first TV newscast on KRSD-TV, NBC affiliate for Rapid City. Eli had been after Norm, the radio newsman, for weeks to get the TV news program going. Our competition, Channel 3 CBS, had their newscast with weather and sports and were clobbering us in the ratings. Norm confided in me that he was terrified at the thought of appearing on camera on live TV! He had been a radio newscaster all his life and quite frankly was not all that photogenic!

Finally Eli had had it! The call came loud and clear—we could all hear every word from the telephone earpiece as Norm held it four feet from his ear! *"Get that [blankety-blank] news program on the [blankety-blank] air [blankety-blank] TONIGHT or you're all fired!"—slam!*

Once again, Norm pleaded, "Paul, you do it, you are a preacher, you have done public speaking. I'm on my knees!"

All we had was a plain old folding card table and a blue tablecloth. We ripped the latest roundup from the UPI teletype service and yours truly had the distinct honor of reading the *very first* newscast for NBC Rapid City! Once again, I thank God there was no way to record that program—it was awful—strictly "amateur night in Dixie," even though we were far north of the Mason-Dixon line.

Eli's wrath was appeased and gradually we added weather and sports. The weathercast was the hardest because you had to stand behind a plate-glass map of the U.S. and write all your figures backward to make them read right for the camera.

❦

And then there were the commercials—am I boring you all? You've got to hear this one. Many a night I was the only one on duty operating master control. The last program was usually the *Late Show*. When the cue marks flashed on the films, I would stop the movie, turn on the studio lights, run like crazy onto the set with a locked-down camera, do the cottage cheese commercial, then dash back to the control booth, and restart the movie! And my staff complains today if we do not have at least four to six cameras and a crew of at least eight or ten! Give me a break! I guess we do produce a little better quality these days, so relax— most jobs are secure! Sometimes I had the luxury of Jan writing out my commercial script on newswire paper and slowly pulling it over her arm as I read the Niagara Cyclo Massage commercial.

One highlight I must tell you about was the time Dr. Oral Roberts came to Rapid City to hold a great crusade for the Sioux Indians. Brother Roberts is part American Indian and for years has held an annual crusade conducted primarily to win Native Americans to Christ. This was really big-time stuff for little old Rapid City. The town, the churches, the media was buzzing. Oral Roberts was simply the most prominent healing evangelist of that day—this was about 1958.

I asked Eli if I could invite Dr. Roberts to be a guest on my "LIVE" newscast and he readily agreed. I believe we could say that the very first Christian TV interview program was aired that night as we turned the TV news into a virtual *Praise the Lord* program. Needless to say, the Indian crusade in the Civic Auditorium was a turn-away crowd, and Dr. Roberts kicked our ratings off the scale that night. Eli groused that we had used up too much time for religious news, but the Good News was out and there was no recalling it! Little did I realize that Dr. Roberts's path and mine would cross again twenty-five years later and that we would have REAL *Praise the Lord* programs—many of them!

❦

Well, children, I could write this whole book about our Rapid City experiences, but I will conclude with the most important— the most exciting—the most blessed event of all!

Much to our dismay, Jan began to wake up each morning very sick, nauseated and vomiting. At first I was very worried, but the ladies at church just smiled and said, "You're going to be a daddy!"

Ah, the wonder and excitement for a young couple as they watch and experience the miracle of new life. I will never forget Jan's look of panic as those first labor pains started, nor the break-neck race to Bennett Memorial Hospital. In those days fathers were not allowed in the delivery room—a senseless rule that has mostly been changed today. My angel, Jan, was a brave little trouper as she passed through the "valley of the shadow of death" to give us Paul F. Crouch Jr. on March 13, 1959.

I will never forget that first glimpse of Paul Jr. as the nurse swabbed his tiny nose and ears with cotton Q-tips. He was squalling his head off, but I felt ten feet tall as I hugged Jan and thanked her for giving me the desire of every father's heart—a son! We packed our new treasure proudly into that same little VW Bug that had carried Jan and me on our first date two years earlier and drove to our little trailer home parked in the middle of a pine tree forest in the Black Hills of South Dakota. Just "Mommy and me and baby makes three"—we were happy in our new heaven!

The next day on my deejay radio show I found a song that said it best: *"It's a boy, it's a joy, it's the first but not the last . . ."* I played that record a dozen or more times, giving Paul Jr.'s name and vital statistics. He was probably the best-known live birth in the history of Rapid City. Eli finally walked into the control room and told me to cut it out!

Ah, the joy and the memories that flood my soul as I recall the Black Hills of South Dakota. In the natural I wish we could have stayed there forever. Father and son could have grown up together like Daniel Boone and Davy Crockett. I would have taken him deer hunting and trout fishing—we would have hiked up Harney Peak and camped out at the base of Mt. Rushmore. But this was the beginning of something much bigger than I could have ever imagined—this was *Television 101*—this was the training ground for what would become a voice like no other—God's voice to a lost and dying world. Yes, *"Hello World"* was coming fast, but that is yet another chapter.

CHAPTER SEVEN

CALIFORNIA, HERE WE COME!

THE ROAD TO CALIFORNIA DETOURED BRIEFLY through—of all places—Muskegon, Michigan. Bernard and Naomi Ridings had received a call and had accepted the pastorate of Central Assembly of God in Muskegon and had asked Jan and me along with our new bundle of joy, Paul Jr., to go with them and continue as assistant pastors. For about two years I really learned the ministry of pastoring, since we were now in full-time ministry. Weddings, funerals, baptisms, choir directing, Sunday school classes, and yes, another ham-radio class! It was in my blood—there was no evading it. I even wrote the FCC for application papers to start a small radio station, but the deacons couldn't catch the vision or the budget!

In retrospect, those two years seemed to be mostly marking time, but we did learn to love some of the most precious saints of

God we had ever met. It was in Muskegon that we first met a young Jim and Tammy Bakker, who were attending Bible school, though we only saw them a few times on home visits during breaks and holidays. Jim's mom and dad, Fern and Raleigh, were pillars in the church, Raleigh being the head usher. Jim's Grandma Irwin was one of the most Christlike ladies I had ever met. Again, only God knew that Jim Bakker and I would meet again, years later, in California.

The whole reason for our moving to Muskegon just may have been for the brief encounter with Jim Bakker, for he and Tammy did indeed make their mark upon our lives and ministry that remains to this very day. How strange and, indeed, sovereign are the crossroads of our lives, but that chapter is coming up!

The really BIG event for Muskegon was—morning sickness number TWO! Our little family was growing! By now Paul Jr. was two and he got very excited along with Jan and me as the big day drew near. I wanted another boy—don't ask me why—I just did. Maybe it was the lines of one of the old songs by Andy Williams that went, *"When you're the father of boys, you worry, but when you're the father of girls, you pray!"* In any case, I got my wish and on October 26, 1961, my number-two son, Matthew Wendell Crouch, discovered America in Hackley Hospital, Muskegon, Michigan.

❦

But Matt was not destined to even remember the place of his birth due to an urgent call one day from Willard Cantelon, a dear minister friend. The scene was actually a very sad one. Jan and I were conducting the funeral of a young father who had been killed by a tragic explosion. The church secretary called me from the platform for what I thought must be another emergency of some kind. But the phone call was electrifying. Willard's voice was excited—"Paul, the Assemblies of God is establishing a TV and Film Production Center out here in Burbank, California . . . "

My heart did flip-flops as I anticipated the next sentence.

"General Superintendent Thomas Zimmerman has asked me to call you to see if you would be willing to move out here and manage it!"

Words could not express the joy that leaped in my spirit! This was it—this was what those ham-radio days were for—KCBI and "Hello World"—my crazy pioneering days at NBC Rapid City—*hallelujah*— my spirit soared! I knew that Willard Cantelon had been pioneering a new TV series for the Assemblies of God. *Men With a Mission* documented miraculous stories from the foreign mission fields. Though pretty crude technically by today's standards, since everything was still shot on 16mm motion-picture film, at least it was now in color.

Willard was purchasing time on secular TV stations to recruit personnel and resources for preaching Christ around the world! "Willard, tell Brother Zimmerman YES, but I have to go. Jan and I have just been called to sing at a funeral that is being conducted in the church right now! I'll call you back in a couple of hours!"

Jan only heard one side of the conversation, but had the general idea of our upcoming move as we stepped back on the platform to sing. I felt pure giddy as we began to sing, *"UNTIL THEN MY HEART WILL GO ON SINGING"*—then I began to feel pure guilt for being so happy as we tried to continue comforting the bereaved. *"UNTIL THEN WITH JOY I'LL CARRY ON . . . "* The song had absolutely opposite meanings for Jan and me and the mourners. "*UNTIL THE DAY MY EYES BEHOLD THAT CITY . . .* "The mourners were thinking of heaven, I was wondering what Burbank would be like! "*UNTIL THE DAY GOD CALLS ME HOME.*"

The song and funeral could not end soon enough for me. Somehow deep in my spirit I knew this was God's next phase for a destiny that was now becoming clearer—GLORY! *California, here we come!*

We said good-bye to some of the dearest people on earth at Central Assembly of God, Muskegon, Michigan, and headed for California. Paul Jr. was two and a half, and Matt was one month old. Uncle Bernie and Aunt Nonie, as Paul Jr. called them, helped us load all our earthly possessions into a small U-Haul trailer as we said a tearful good-bye on Thanksgiving Day 1961. We felt a little like the "Beverly Hillbillies" as we rolled west toward the Golden State!

Again, I could write a whole book just about Burbank and this wonderful phase God had moved us into. For nearly five years Jan and I helped pioneer a department of the Assemblies of God that continues to this day. We produced records, tapes, filmstrips, and motion pictures for the Assemblies of God and several other denominations, from church-growth documentaries like *Cincinnati Breakthrough* to *Light for the Lost* motion pictures that we shot in many foreign nations. Jan did secretarial duties and, of course, makeup as we filmed many productions in our studio at 3805 W. Magnolia in "Beautiful Downtown Burbank." We even did some work for the U.S. Army and their series called *The Big Picture.*

It was exciting work since we also got to meet a number of

Hollywood stars and even joined the Hollywood Christian group. We found to our amazement that there were many well-known Hollywood personalities who knew and loved the Lord Jesus. Stars like Jane Russell, Pat Boone, Ty Hardin, Roy Rogers, Dale Evans, Art Linkletter, and many others met regularly for prayer and Bible study. *Dear Lord,* I thought, *the folks back home will never believe that there are REAL Christians in the entertainment business out here in Hollywood!* Jan and I were delighted and flattered to be asked to joined this esteemed group.

I suppose our biggest assignment was to produce the fiftieth anniversary motion picture that traced the origins of the Assemblies of God from its first founding and General Council in Hot Springs, Arkansas, in 1914. By 1964 it had become the largest Pentecostal denomination in the world as well as the fastest growing. I was proud to know that my dad, Andrew Crouch, was one of the founders of the Assemblies of God and is pictured in the first historic photograph with men like J. R. Flower, E. N. Bell, J. W. Welch, and many other well-known ministers in the Assembly circles. *Like a River* was the title of this historic production and it is still a teaching film for Assemblies colleges and churches.

Of course, *A Child Is Wanting* was my favorite production since it documented the tragic stories but also the wonderful rescue of the children at the Hot Springs orphanage. Believe it or not, yours truly *(I was young then)* actually played a bit part in the courtroom scene shot in a real Burbank courtroom with Byron Morrow and Vic Perrin, who was well known at the time for his role in the Jack Webb *Dragnet* TV series.

Yes, Burbank was indeed the vital next phase of this most unusual college of "hard knocks" that God was putting Jan and me through.

But all good things must come to an end, and that day came when the officials at Springfield decided to move the TV and Film Production Center from Burbank back to Springfield, Missouri, the denomination's headquarters. After thought and much prayer, Jan and I agreed that we were to remain in California. It was one of the most difficult decisions of our lives. After all, Springfield was my hometown, all my friends were there, my own precious mother was there—my heart was pulled toward home, but the Holy Spirit said, "Stay"!

I do not need to tell my boys much about our next phase of "schooling" in Corona, California since it was there their most memorable childhood and school days were experienced. As we were saying good-bye to Burbank, Dr. William J. Roberts called me to ask if I would consider managing his radio station in Corona, a suburb of the sprawling Southern California metroplex. Dr. Roberts was a well-known radio pioneer and pastor, having been one of the founders of FEBC, the Far East Broadcasting Company, sending shortwave Christian radio into Asia for many years. We accepted and for the next five years I learned FCC law, business management skills, and rough and tough competition, with dozens of stations vying for the scarce advertising dollars in the market. This was "graduate school" time—it was make-it-or-go-broke time. There were no safety nets—you got out there and hustled your program and advertising time for as little as a *"dollar a holler,"* as the old joke went.

KREL, Corona, California, was owned by a small group of Christian partners and we did broadcast some religious programs, but by and large it was a pure commercial venture. After two years the partners were pleased enough with my performance that a 10 percent block of corporate stock was given to me as a bonus! Wonder of wonders—I was now a radio station owner!

Jan became "Mrs. Civic Corona." From president of the PTA to chairman of the Mayor's Ball, she worked hard to help make KREL the community leader—FCC public service at its best! I'm sure Paul Jr. remembers dressing up, at about age eight, in that classic page-boy outfit and reading the official invitation to the City Council to attend the Mayor's Ball. He was a doll and made the front page of the *Corona Courier!*

I'm sure Matt remembers coming home from school starving, because his teacher refused to give him his lunch, which was delivered late because he forgot it. *Boy howdy,* heads rolled as Jan and the PTA *"hit the beaches"!* It was well-known that the whole school lunch program changed as a group of angry mothers descended on the superintendent of schools to demand better food, and that the kids be allowed to eat inside rather than sweltering or freezing on outside benches because the teachers did not want the mess inside. God was surely toughening us both up for the REAL battles ahead. Yes, Garrettson Avenue School may never be the same since President Jan and her compatriots launched their "D-Day" on elementary education in Corona, California.

Our little family had many happy, learning, growing-up days in Corona, but still there was that deep inner gnawing in my spirit that even Corona was only more preparation for some greater calling—a yet unknown destiny that somehow lay just ahead.

CHAPTER EIGHT

THE MIRACLE BEGINS!

THE MIRACLE BIRTH OF TBN REALLY BEGAN IN 1971 with a call from Ray Schoch, pastor of Faith Center Church in Glendale, California. He had launched an FM radio station and had just been successful in acquiring an FCC permit for a UHF TV station licensed to San Bernardino, California. The idea of a whole TV station devoted 100 percent to Christian programming was a radical new concept, but Pastor Ray was a great man of faith and finally fought it through and got KHOF-TV Channel 30 on the air!

The problem was that San Bernardino was about sixty miles east of Glendale, which was virtually out of our range in Glendale. We could not even pick up the signal at the church in Glendale. It did, however, cover much of the greater Southern California area.

Both the radio and new TV station were struggling financially. FM was relatively new for radio, and UHF—well, in those days very few TV home receivers were even wired to receive it. You had to get that little black box that sat on top of the set—remember? We estimated that only about 20 percent of the homes in Southern California could even receive UHF Channel 30.

Pastor Schoch's call to come and manage his stations came at a God-ordained time. I had just sold my interest in the Corona radio station, and Jan and I were simply waiting on the Lord in the new home we had just purchased for $38,500 in Orange County, California. It's a lot lonelier since our boys moved out, but it still holds many wonderful memories for all of us. As Edgar Guest wrote, "It takes a heap of living in a house to make it home." Well, after thirty-three years of laughter and tears, that little house in Newport Beach will ever be remembered as home to Jan and me! I will ever know that God led us to that home since it was only about ten minutes from 111 West Dyer Road in Santa Ana—an address that was to become home to . . . but again, I'm getting ahead of my story.

Now, I must hurry because we are coming to that rendezvous with destiny—the culmination of those many years of testing and training—the purpose, I believe, for which I was born. My children, there is nothing more important in all of life than to find your purpose—God's purpose for you! How many live sad, depressed, and unfulfilled lives simply because they did not find God's perfect plan for their lives. That line sounds almost like a super-spiritual cliché, but God really does have an exciting, happy, gloriously fulfilled life for everyone.

But how does one find it? Well, that subject deserves a book all its own and many, of course, have been written about it, but let me give you three important clues before moving on. First of all, God says in Jeremiah 29:13, *"And ye shall seek me, and find me, when ye shall search for me with all your heart."*

Secondly, make your important decisions in life only after prayer and in agreement with your prayer partner.

And here is a final word: Paul says in Colossians 3:15, *"And let the peace of God rule in your hearts."* I have learned that if my spirit is not at peace when faced with a decision, I simply wait. When the decision is right, you will know—God's perfect peace will rule in your spirits.

But back to my story.

❦

I accepted Pastor Ray Schoch's invitation, and for two years we pioneered Christian TV—this radical new concept of a whole TV station programmed 100 percent for the Lord. *What a challenge— where do you get the programs?* Well, the answer was easy—you produce them—but the doing was next to impossible! Back in Rapid City it was a snap. NBC sent us 90 percent of our programming. All we had to do was a little news (*remember that one?*), weather, and sports. So, who's going to do a Bible study . . . a children's show . . . a music program? We did have Pastor Schoch's Sunday services and what a great preacher he was. I learned more about raw faith from this precious saint than all of my previous schooling. Bible school teaches *about* faith—Pastor Ray *walked* it and *lived* it!

So we went to work. Brother Willard Pierce, a precious elder on the staff, taught a daily Bible study, and how rich was his teaching. Believe it or not, I actually did my very first *Behind the Scenes* programs on Channel 30. It must have been my love for news born in Rapid City! Pat Robertson sent us the *Jim and Tammy* children's show. Remember that one? Jim Bakker, and his wife Tammy, pioneered a great children's program for several years.

Things were going great and Pastor Ray advised us that we should move up to Glendale, since I was driving fifty miles one way to work every day. We agreed and began a house search nearer to the church and TV offices. We also began having TV rallies, since our audience was growing and word was getting around that *CHRISTIAN TELEVISION* was on the air in Southern California.

By now we were actually on from about 5 P.M. to 10 P.M. Even five hours a day was a challenge, but everything was going and growing—even the finances were up dramatically—and it seemed that Jan and I had finally found our place: a wonderful, Spirit-filled church that owned a radio and TV station, with nowhere to go but up!

It was March 10, 1973—we had decided to invade even Hollywood, California! For weeks we promoted it on radio and TV. We rented the Hollywood High School auditorium that seated about one thousand people. We were so excited—oh, how we hoped the partners and TV viewers would all turn out—and they did! It was glorious—the room was filled with enthusiastic, live-wire, on-fire partners! The cream of the Christian crop—they proved it—having to put up with some of the sorriest, poorly produced TV programs ever! They knew it but loved us any way—we were pioneering 100 percent Christian television together!

Doug Oldham was our special guest singer and speaker. He had recently recorded a hit Christian song that was sweeping the nation—"THE KING IS COMING"—remember that one? What a song and what a blessing it brought to the whole Body of Christ. We sang, shouted, shared testimonies, and praised the Lord. I shared the vision of not just one, but many TV stations—yes, a network to preach Christ from coast to coast.

When we prayed the benediction and said good night, Jan and I were glowing! Hundreds of wonderful partners had lingered to shake hands, greet us, and congratulate us for the great new blessing of Christian television.

❦

Surely this was it—surely we were settled and secure in the ministry and calling that God had placed upon our lives. As we drove out of the parking lot of Hollywood High School that night we were higher than the proverbial kite . . . when God spoke! He spoke as clearly and distinctly as I had ever heard His voice. He said, *"Paul, I release you from your ministry at KHOF-TV."*

An atom bomb going off at that moment would not have surprised me more! I was thunderstruck—for several moments I could not even speak! Finally I turned to Jan and said, "Honey, you will never believe what God has just spoken to me!"

Without a moment's hesitation she replied, "I know. I heard Him, too—God has just released you from your ministry here at KHOF."

It took several more moments for the enormity of this immediate confirmation of God to register and settle in on me. Even at this earliest stage of what was indeed to become the final phase of our work and ministry, God had confirmed His word to us scripturally: *"that in the mouth of two or three witnesses every word may be established"* (Matthew 18:16). Not much else was spoken as we drove the hour or so back home. Like Mary, the mother of Jesus, we pondered in our hearts, with awe, the word of the Lord that had been spoken to us both simultaneously!

In my mind the big question was: *Now what? Why would God change anything that was going so well? Another TV station perhaps?* We had longed for a station right in Los Angeles that would really cover all of the 12 million-plus population of Southern California. *Maybe that is it,* I mused. But then I remembered that all of the TV stations allocated by the FCC were either on the air or under construction. Besides, I knew that the last sale of a TV station in this number-two TV market had cost the buyer $1,650,000! How could Jan and I ever hope to raise that kind of money to buy a TV station?

For several days we interceded to God for direction. Finally, in prayer one day, the Lord reminded me of a fairly new TV station that had signed on the air about six months earlier. With fear and trepidation I finally phoned the owner, Bill Myers, to inquire on the status of Channel 46 which, by the way, was located on Mt. Wilson, next door to all the main network TV stations for Los

Angeles. I could hardly believe what I heard. He explained that his station had not been successful and that he had been forced to sign it *OFF THE AIR!*

My heart did a few more flip-flops—I tried to sound only mildly interested as I made an appointment to discuss the possible acquisition of his station. The appointment was not for several days, so Jan and I continued to fast and pray for God's perfect direction and will.

A few nights later at the altar of our church, God began the molding process in our lives. It was an anointed time with an unusual conclusion to the service. Jan and I usually prayed together, but for whatever reason that night I knelt on one side of the church and she knelt on the other side. Unknown to either of us at the time, we were both literally "slain in the spirit." We personally experienced those *"groanings which cannot be uttered"* (Romans 8:26), as the Holy Spirit made intercession through us. Suddenly, without warning, our pastor, Syvelle Phillips, moving by divine revelation, leaped to his feet and declared, *"A new television ministry is being born!"*

It felt like a mighty bolt of electricity crackled through the air as wave after wave of glory swept through the room and into our very souls! We had told Pastor Phillips nothing of our word from the Lord; he only knew that Jan and I were praying about some personal matter concerning our lives. We lingered at that altar till way past midnight, singing, weeping, and praising the Lord.

Mark and Diana Yashuhara, the "Hawaiians," were there that night and their songs, anointed with the glory of the Lord, filled us with a wonder and sweetness I shall never forget. Here, in only a few short days, had come the THIRD confirmation of this divine call. At the conclusion of that glorious service, sweet little Grandmother Avery met me at the door as we were leaving. You wonder why we talk about and praise God for our grandmas on the air? Let me tell you, if it were not for the *women*—and *especially* those grandmas, those *"mothers in Israel"*—there would be no Christian TV! When we all get to heaven, we'll surely see that it was the "GRAMMAS"—Jan's group of *"GOD'S RADICAL ARMY OF MOUNTAIN MOVERS AGAINST SATAN,"* who have prayed us through every impossible situation!

The third confirmation was this gift: Grandma Avery reached for my hand and pressed a crumpled bill into it. Looking deep into my eyes, she said, "Paul, you'll need some finances to get started—it's not much, but God will multiply it!"

I hugged her and thanked her and later reflected that Grandma Avery's five-dollar bill was the FIRST love gift that we would receive! Today, Grandma Avery is dancing on streets of gold, sharing in the more than 20 million souls who have received Christ through *her* Christian TV network!

Looking back thirty years, now I can tell you: this was IT—this was truly the beginning of HIS miracle! But had we known the tortured trail that lay just ahead—oh, God, that comes next. Let's move on.

CHAPTER NINE

YE SHALL SAY TO THAT MOUNTAIN

EVENTS WERE NOW MOVING AT A DIZZYING SPEED as God began moving all the people, places, and things into place for the birth of His new television ministry. By now it was clear that our whole lives and direction were changing. With very mixed emotions I handed my resignation to Pastor Ray Schoch, who seemed very distressed by my decision. Why would I leave when all was going so well? Indeed, it seemed to everyone at Faith Center that we had just broken through, that Christian TV was finally over the hump and on the way! All I could tell Pastor Ray was that God had spoken—that He was calling me to a path unknown.

With tears in his eyes, Pastor Ray finally spoke. "Paul, if God has spoken, you must obey. If you stayed, we would both be making a grave mistake and would be missing the will of God."

Sadly, in the days that followed, many at Faith Center misunderstood our new calling. Harsh accusations were made that I was out to harm Faith Center—that I was deliberately seeking to start a competing TV station in the same market. I was even accused of stealing the TV mailing list which, by the way, I did not even have access to since it was held by a large mailing firm in Los Angeles.

As I told you earlier, the wounds and hurts of your brothers and sisters are the worst spiritual pain you will ever feel. Jan and I were devastated and nearly gave up in these early beginning stages of our new, and as yet unknown, journey. One night in prayer, with the pain of false accusations swirling all around us, God gave us a precious word of encouragement from Hebrews 11:8:

> *By faith Abraham, when he was called to go out into a place which he should after receive for an inheritance, obeyed; and he went out, not knowing whither he went.*

Jan and I held on to that word and each other as we vowed to move on into the unknown.

A few days later we finally met with Mr. Myers and worked out a contract to purchase time on his TV station so that we could sign on right away. We agreed to continue working out the final purchase agreement for the license of the entire TV station. In the meantime, $10,000 a month would pay for four hours a night and would enable him to sign KBSA-TV Channel 46 back on the air. With a hard gulp, I signed the contract!

❦

About this same time God led us to a group of Christian busi-
nessmen who owned an industrial complex of buildings in Santa
Ana. A computer firm had just moved out of 111 West Dyer
Road—remember that address? Dear Lord, I will never forget it!
Jan and I still drive by occasionally and get goose bumps—you'll
understand why as we move on.

Mr. Ward Vanguard, a member of our church, was one of the
partners and had heard of our new venture through friends. Since
Channel 46 had no studio, only a transmitter, he explained that
his building just might be a possible new studio home for the TV
station. As we walked through the empty rooms, I could hardly
believe my eyes: plenty of offices, large rooms with smaller
glassed-in rooms for studios and control rooms, heavy electrical
circuits, and oversized air-conditioning for hot TV lights. God
had designed it perfectly for a TV station! And, to clinch the deal,
the owners gave us the first three months rent-free!

On April 24, 1973, I signed another contract—this time a
lease valued at more than $250,000 with no guarantees or collat-
eral of any kind. In retrospect, this transaction stands out as one
of the great miracles that God did for us.

❦

The ink was hardly dry on the paper when I looked up and saw
our car come roaring up to the front door of the leasing office. Jan
jumped out, squealing, "Call Chicago in ten minutes . . . call

Chicago in ten minutes!" When I finally got her calmed down, the story tumbled out. Somehow, news of our new station had reached Chicago and Mr. Jack Teas, a millionaire, wanted to offer financial backing. I couldn't dial fast enough and sure enough, Mr. Teas answered. With only the briefest explanation, our new "benefactor" was actually on his way to California!

When Mr. Teas arrived two days later, he looked more like Al Capone's bodyguard than the benevolent donor we had envisioned. For several days we discussed financing arrangements, loans, percentages of interest, collateral, and guarantees. At every lunch he always outfumbled us, and I picked up the check with our fast-dwindling resources.

Here we learned a painful but valuable lesson. Hear me, everyone—do not depend upon the arm of the flesh! More important, we had forgotten to pray for God's direction or for the discerning of spirits which God gives us through His Holy Spirit. What followed was a total waste of our time and an even worse disruption of our work. We nearly lost our entire direction as Mr. Teas turned out to be full of hot air and had no money! God had a perfect plan for His TV station and it did not include any phony millionaires! God wanted His little people, from the children to the grandmas, to have a part in his new TV station! Praise the Lord!

Now it was time to put some work with our faith. For days we scraped tile off the floors of the main studio rooms to make a smooth surface for cameras to roll on, hung lights, and hooked up equipment. So many wonderful volunteers with special talents began showing up. Everything and everyone we needed came and always just at the right time. A secretary arrived, carrying her own typewriter, a carpet layer just as the set needed carpet, carpenters, electricians, furniture movers—it was truly miraculous—God just sent them to us and always at precisely the right time as work progressed.

One day we needed a gas line moved that was in the way of the lights that were being hung. We formed a little circle of prayer just as we had done so many times before. "Lord, we need a specialist for this job and we don't have the money to hire him . . ." The words were barely out of our mouths when through the door walked Bill Crandall. On his uniform was a patch that read "Southern California Gas Company"! We laughed and cried and praised the Lord, as Bill, tools and all, closed valves, cut pipe, and moved the line out of the way for the TV lights.

Finally, we were nearing SIGN-ON! The final step was the microwave unit. This piece of equipment sent picture and sound from our nearly remodeled studio in Santa Ana to the transmitter on top of Mt. Wilson, almost fifty miles north. From there, the signal was rebroadcast to the vast Southern California megalopolis. Again, a very specialized skill was needed. We began to pray— "Lord, where will we find a microwave engineer—whom shall we call?" And, as God is my witness, within minutes the phone rang. The caller? You guessed it—a microwave engineer!

❦

In a matter of hours he was there with four more engineers. They worked for three days, trying to get the TV signal from our studio to Mt. Wilson. Something seemed to be blocking the signal because nothing, not even a glimmer of the picture, was coming through. Maybe something was wrong with the equipment; after all, the station had been off the air for more than six months. So the engineers brought the receiver down from Mt. Wilson to the studio. They placed the transmitter a few feet from the receiver, turned on the power, and bingo! The picture was perfect. Nothing was wrong with the equipment.

Finally, in desperation, we called the telephone company—they provided microwave services for many clients. The message caused our hearts to sink. "Forget it!" was the word. They told us either the Whittier hills or possibly a part of Mt. Wilson itself was in the way. They had tried microwave shots from several spots in Santa Ana and it just couldn't be done!

Now we were desperate—we were running out of time—the FCC authority to remain off the air expired on Monday, May 28, 1973, and this was Saturday! The license could be lost if we did not meet the deadline and sign the station on that Monday! Once again, we had no one to turn to but the Lord.

I remember how discouraged everyone was. Again, it looked like we were finished. I really didn't know why at the time, but I walked around to the back of the studio and began climbing the steel ladder to the roof where the microwave dish was installed.

❧

I honestly did not notice that Paul Jr. and Matt were with me as I slowly inched my way to the roof. I guess I was in such a fog I was not aware of their being there. They reminded me, even as I was writing this account, that they had both witnessed this amazing encounter with God. How thankful I am that they were there, not only to vouch for the truth of this miracle, but far more important, to know that there is a God in heaven and that He really does move mountains!

Everyone knew that we were at another standstill—another crisis—another test of our faith. NO PICTURE—and we had to be on the air within forty-eight hours! Tears began rolling down my face. I reached out and laid my hands on the cold curved steel of the microwave dish—"Father, You said that if we would have *faith even as a grain of mustard seed, you could SAY to THAT MOUNTAIN—be thou removed and be cast into the sea . . .*'" His holy presence descended upon the roof of that studio, and somehow I KNEW that my Heavenly Father had heard and answered my prayer. I dried my eyes and climbed back down the ladder. As I rounded the studio corner, I bumped into Jan, who was crying and very discouraged. She asked where I had been. I explained that I had just had a talk with my Father up on the roof and that everything was going to be all right.

The engineers were very tired after twelve hours of hard labor, trying since early morning, to get the TV signal through to Mt. Wilson. They were packing up to leave and everyone was very discouraged. I asked the chief engineer if they would all come back and try just one more time the next morning, which was Sunday. Incidentally, this engineer had borrowed twenty dollars from me and was refusing to pay it back! He said, "Well, Mr. Crouch, it's your money"—(*how true*)—"We'll give it one more shot, but personally I think it's a waste of time!" I didn't tell him at the time, but our money was virtually exhausted.

The next morning, we were all there at eight o'clock sharp. But this time something was different—there was electricity in the air! For several minutes circuits warmed up, transformers hummed, and final adjustments were made. The engineer up on Mt Wilson was on the phone with the chief and all of us in the studio. Suddenly, a shout came from the telephone—we could hear it clear across the room! *"We've got it!"* he cried. *"We've got the picture and it's as clear as NBC!"*

All heaven broke loose in our little control room at 111 West Dyer Road in Santa Ana that Sunday morning! We laughed, we cried, we shouted!

The engineers were thunderstruck—they could not believe what they were hearing. The chief was a chain-smoker. He had kept the air blue with his smoke that whole week, testing the patience and sanctification of all of us. As he stared at the TV screen that Sunday morning, his cigarette dropped to the floor, he crushed it under his shoe, and never smoked in that little studio building again. We all knew from that moment on we were standing on holy ground. By the way, he also reached into his pocket and paid back the twenty dollars that he owed me!

Yes, we all are witnesses. God moved a mountain for us and we will ever know that this was not just a spiritual mountain— this was a real dirt, rock, and tree mountain! Oh, praise the Lord! And for thirty years now, the TBN signal has been passing through that "cleft in the rock" that our God carved for us.

There really is NOTHING TOO HARD for our God! Yes, He made it possible for us to meet the FCC deadline just in time!

❦

Yes, the miracle really began the very next night on Monday, May 28, 1973. Only three months from the time God first spoke to Jan and me, TRINITY BROADCASTING NETWORK was ON THE AIR, lifting up Jesus with "LET'S JUST PRAISE THE LORD!" Yes, a TV station that had taken Bill Myers ten years to get permits through and build, by a miracle of God's will, was back on the air with 100 percent Christian programming in only three months!

That very first night we were on the air, telephone calls came in from all over Southern California. How they even knew we were on is a mystery and a miracle all its own! Hundreds of God's wonderful people joined in just to "Praise the Lord" with us for this mighty new miracle of God. Many of the callers could not even see the picture, since Channel 46 was a very low-power station. Many said, "All we can see is a snowstorm, but we can hear you just fine! Keep up the good work, we are praying for you!"

An interesting sidelight to all of the excitement of Channel 46 coming on the air occurred that next Sunday at our church, First Assembly of Santa Ana. A fiery new evangelist from Texas had come to begin revival meetings. Dwight and Zonelle Thompson brought a whole new dimension to what we call PENTECOSTAL! Dwight was a refreshing infusion of new life to our *"California"* style of worship. The church was packed every night, but our new Christian TV channel was also on the air each night.

The next Sunday morning Sister Gertrude Pomeroy, one of the pillars of the church, came up to me and I could tell that something was wrong! "Paul Crouch"—I knew when she called me by my full name, it was coming! "Why would you start your TV station right in the middle of Dwight Thompson's REVIVAL?" You see, she was torn—wanting to come to church, but also terribly excited by the new TV channel! I assured her that this dilemma would soon pass and finally appeased her by agreeing to come to her home to install a proper TV antenna so that she could get a clearer picture of Channel 46. We made our peace with Sister Pomeroy and she continued as one of our staunchest partners until her home going in 1992.

Yes, victory rang all across Southern California that historic night that TBN signed on the air, and Dwight's revival was also a great blessing and success! But testing time was just ahead. *Buckle up, everyone*—there's a bad curve coming just up the road!

CHAPTER TEN

"YOU HAVE GIVEN ME NOTHING!"

WHILE TIME HAS PROVEN THAT TBN WAS GOD'S ultimate goal for Jan and me, and while it is now evident that most of our efforts and experiences were training and preparation for this goal, there was still a lot of *postgraduate* work that God had to take us through. Incidentally, that training is still going on in all of our lives.

My next great lesson was one I did not even know I needed. If you have not learned this lesson, you can save yourselves a lot of pain and sorrow by reading this chapter very carefully! Get a firm grip on your pocketbook, and then be prepared to—let me explain.

We had agreed to pay Mr. Myers $10,000 a month for the four hours a day of airtime, while still negotiating the purchase of the whole station. Jan and I had invested our $20,000 in this new venture! This was profit from the sale of my interest in the Corona radio station, plus our entire life savings. We had bought lumber for sets, paid the utility deposits, installed telephones, rented some TV equipment, plus paid Mr. Myers for the first few days of airtime. Three days after the euphoria of signing on the air, our funds were nearly exhausted.

God had sent Jim and Tammy Bakker back into our lives shortly before we had signed on the air. They had just recently left their work and ministry with Pat Robertson back in Portsmouth, Virginia. As I told you earlier, we had met Jim and Tammy back at Jim's home church in Muskegon, Michigan, never dreaming that our paths would cross again twelve years later in California. After much prayer and planning we entered into a ministry partnership in this new venture—I was chairman of the board and Jim was president.

The Bakkers had arrived much like Jan and I had arrived in California—pulling a trailer with all their worldly possessions on board, and broke! While they had no money to invest, they brought something just as valuable: simple, childlike faith in God, which was a source of strength and inspiration to us all. Our boys will remember that they were dispossessed from their bedroom for a month or so as Jim and Tammy moved in with daughter Tammy Sue and Biscuit, their tiny terrier pup.

Mr. Myers did not believe in credit, so he demanded an additional $3,000 before he would sign the station back on the air that third night! I recall turning to Jim that day and asking, "Now what?" Jim and I prayed for God's help and direction when in the door came my pastor, Syvelle Phillips! We quickly explained our predicament to him and asked if he would intercede with Mr. Myers on our behalf. He did, and after a lengthy discussion and the payment of our very last $1,000, Mr. Myers agreed to sign the station on for one more night.

My emotions were so drained after that meeting, I knew it would be meaningless for me to try and face the TV cameras that night. Pastor Phillips said, "Paul, it is time to tell the people exactly what our need is." He agreed to host the program that night and I headed home to pray. As I drove toward home, I began to cry out my complaint to the Lord. "Why does it have to be so hard, Lord? Why do we have to suffer so much? Lord, You have provided everything we have needed up to this very moment—what does this all mean?"

I literally pounded on the steering wheel of my car as I headed up MacArthur Boulevard toward home. As I wept before the Lord, that still, small voice spoke again—so sweetly and clearly this time that it startled me. The Lord said, *"Paul, it is difficult because you have not GIVEN Me anything."*

This message startled me even more! "What do You mean, Lord?" I protested. "I have given You everything—my ministry at KHOF and Faith Center, my life, my talents, EVEN our $20,000 life savings!"

The Lord spoke again and said, *"Son, you did not GIVE Me your savings; you only LOANED them to Me."*

Ah, it was true! The Lord knows everything—even the secret

thoughts of our hearts. I had taken a promissory note back for the money I had placed in the new ministry. I had only *LOANED* our money to God. Now, He said, "I want you to *GIVE ME* your savings!"

Well, for me this was an awesome request. Didn't God know how *hard* we had worked for years to save this money? Didn't He know how we had sacrificed and even gone *without* to put this money aside for our future? But without my really realizing it, money had become a hindrance to my spiritual growth—perhaps even a *god* of sorts—and the Lord was asking me to give it up— ALL of it!

I struggled with the decision all the way home and finally, as I literally fell across the bed, I said, "All right, Lord. I will make this bargain with You. If You will cause Your people to give an equal amount—*TONIGHT, on television*—I vow to *GIVE* it *ALL* to You!"

In utter exhaustion, I picked up the telephone and called the station. By now, a full-fledged telethon was under way. Pastor Phillips and Jan were pouring out their hearts to the viewers, telling of our vision and need at TBN. An unusual anointing of the Holy Spirit was upon Pastor Phillips as the opportunity for God's people to OWN their very own TV station poured from his spirit.

Somehow I reached Jan, who was also one of the telephone prayer partners. I said, "Honey, God has spoken to me again." I told her what the word had been and also what I had promised the Lord. I said, "Tell Pastor Phillips that a pledge for $20,000 has come tonight from SOMEONE who loves Christian television very much, but ONLY if God's people will match it with an equal amount TONIGHT."

There was a long pause on the other end of the phone as Jan began to weep softly. She knew better than anyone the battle that was raging within my very soul. My mind was in such turmoil by then, I really do not remember all that was said between us, but I do remember Jan's last word to me over the phone—"I love you, sweetheart," and she was gone.

❧

In a moment I watched, transfixed, as Jan slipped onto the TV studio set, tears streaming down her face, and handed Pastor Phillips the message. The challenge was given and the phones began to *ring and ring and ring!* All heaven came down as God's beautiful people began to call. In less than one hour they had not only matched the challenge, but there was a *$10,000 surplus!*

Yes, after only three nights on the air, on a station that had been dark for more than six months—God spoke to His wonderful people to give more than $50,000. And since the need was so urgent, many actually drove down to the studio to personally deliver their gifts to THEIR TV STATION. All praise to HIS wonderful name! The "Red Sea" had parted and we were walking on dry ground!

Without really realizing it at the time, I had put into motion one of God's most powerful laws—the law of giving and receiving—sowing and reaping. Years later John Avanzini, one of the greatest teachers on giving, would explain and refine these powerful truths from the Word of God for all of us: "*GIVE and it shall be given . . .*"

But here is the most valuable lesson that I learned and now pass on to you with all joy. From that night until now, neither Jan and I, nor TBN has *EVER* suffered an impossible need! I will ever know that our obedience to God that awesome night surely broke through some impenetrable spiritual barrier and released God's glorious provision upon everything that we have attempted to do for HIM! Thirty-, sixty-, and one hundredfold blessing is, indeed, a glorious truth and blessing for those who will simply obey the word of the Lord! Thirty years later I can testify to you that every bill is paid and TBN has *ZERO* capital debt! We literally *"owe no man any thing, but to love one another . . . ,"* as Paul admonished us in Romans 13:8.

One of the pledges that night came from a most blessed and unusual source. A missionary couple, Robin and Marva Farnsworth, had recently returned from New Guinea on furlough. They had been working for more than eight years in the most primitive disease- and mosquito-infested jungles of the world as Bible translators with Wycliffe. The privation and physical pain they and their three children had suffered was clearly seen in their drawn faces.

Brother Farnsworth met me the next day at the door of TBN and said, "Paul, God has spoken to me and I must give you the balance of our travel fund for our new TV station." He held out a check with a trembling hand. "God will supply our needs, I know. Please take this with all our love."

My heart nearly burst within me as I looked at this thin, little man with the scars of physical and spiritual battle so evident upon him, standing there before me seeking to minister to my need. Tears welled up in my eyes as I opened the check—it was $1,480. "Oh, Brother Farnsworth, no," I cried, "I cannot take your travel funds!"

As I spoke a look of intense physical pain came over his drawn face. He replied sternly, "Paul, *God* told me to do this. I must obey the Lord! You can't rob me of this blessing. You have to take it." With that he pressed the check into my hands.

My children, if you have ever wondered why God is blessing TBN, look back at the precious seed that was planted by so many faithful servants of God like the Farnsworths. They so beautifully exemplify the word in Psalms 126:6:

> *He that goeth forth and weepeth, bearing precious seed, shall doubtless come again with rejoicing, bringing his sheaves with him.*

This precious missionary family proved this by their blessed example. Shortly after the miraculous birth of TBN, they returned to the jungles of New Guinea to continue their unsung task of translating the Holy Scriptures into the language of that needy nation. But someday they, too, will rejoice around the throne of God with the millions who have accepted Christ as Savior through this great voice called TBN!

CHAPTER ELEVEN

IN PERILS OF BRETHREN

THE SUMMER OF 1973 MOVED BY SWIFTLY. THESE were busy months as Jim and Tammy and Jan and I labored hard to establish what we prayed would be a solid foundation for the new TV station and ministry. But as fall approached, it became very evident that trouble was on the horizon.

The key pastors of the area and church leaders really did not take our efforts too seriously at these early stages. Much to our disappointment, we soon discovered that many were not at all supportive of this radical new concept—a whole TV station devoted to 100 percent Christian programming. Jan and I were so very naive in assuming that the Christian leaders would welcome this new tool for evangelism with open arms. There were, of course, notable exceptions. For example, our own pastor, Syvelle

Phillips, and Pastor John Hinkle of Christ Church in Los Angeles; Pastor Leroy Saunders of North Hollywood Assembly of God; Pastor Dan Raculia of the Buena Park Community Church; Robert Schuller of Garden Grove Community Church; plus a few others.

Thank God that the people, the Body of Christ, did open their hearts and their pocketbooks, as I explained earlier; but the church leadership in general—well, that was another story. Their suspicion and ultimate rejection of our work was a source of great dismay and sorrow to all of us. I will always believe that the fear, which has now clearly turned out to be unfounded, was that television would be a powerful financial drain on the finances of the churches. For this, and perhaps other reasons, many churches and Christian leaders actually became hostile to this fledgling new ministry.

Jim and I were finally approached by several Christian leaders from the Southern California region. Each of them had a strong opinion on just how the TV station should be managed and operated. Some wanted, even requested, to be elected to the board of directors of TBN. Ralph Wilkerson, pastor of Melodyland Christian Center, was one example. His church had just built a new mobile-TV production truck and finally agreed to loan some of their equipment to us in exchange for program time and a seat on the board of directors. We needed the equipment assistance so desperately that we agreed and voted to place Pastor Ralph on the board.

Ultimately, he began to host some of the *Praise the Lord* programs and finally suggested that we move the whole station over to Melodyland Christian Center, arguing that this would save the considerable rent money which, by now, we were paying to the owners of 111 W. Dyer Road. He was, in effect, suggesting that we make TBN an extension of his church.

We knew this would be a mistake that we felt could actually harm the ministry if it were related to any one church exclusively.

Finally, my own pastor, Syvelle Phillips, feeling more and more left out of the progress and planning of the station, called Jim Bakker and me to a private meeting. His words were harsh and direct. He warned us that if we were to be associated with any church, it should be his—after all, Jan and I were members there and the real vision was actually birthed at the altars of First Assembly! He was also critical of some of the mini-fund-raising telethons that we had conducted from time to time that summer, stating that we were asking too frequently for money. He also was not in agreement with some of the guests and musicians whom we had been inviting to minister on the *Praise the Lord* program, which Jim and I had been alternately hosting. Finally, he exclaimed in conclusion, "You are running this ministry all wrong—you are heading it for the gutter!"

We were stunned and devastated by this critical evaluation from one we had leaned on and respected so totally during the early birth pangs of TBN.

In an effort to appease the many voices that were overwhelming us, we finally agreed to enlarge our board of directors even more. Ward Vanguard, a member of First Assembly, was added at the suggestion of Pastor Phillips. Ralph Wilkerson also suggested a Christian attorney, Norman Juggert, who was doing much of

Melodyland's legal work. (Thirty years later, I can thank Ralph for this suggestion, since Norm served faithfully and selflessly through thick and thin—mountain peaks and valleys—as secretary/treasurer for TBN for over twenty-five years. His staunch Lutheran-German roots were a continual source of stability and wise counsel through the years. Only recently was Norm forced to resign for health reasons.)

As a result of this cacophony of voices and demands from many quarters, Jim Bakker and I, who had worked as a team in the early formative days of the ministry, began to grow further and further apart in the concept and goals of the ministry. Part of this distancing was basically a philosophical difference in several areas, but primarily in the financial area. Jim was much more the creative and artistic talent—I was the tightfisted fiscal conservative. Jim wanted to build expensive and beautiful sets. He wanted to immediately begin buying time to syndicate the *Praise the Lord* program to secular TV stations across America. He invited friends and former associates from back East to join the staff and begin production on several new programs. Much of this was done without consulting the board or even myself, who was not only the chairman of the board, but also general manager of the business affairs of the TV station.

I recall one humorous incident on one of the minithons that Jim and I were conducting. Mr. Ward Vanguard, who, you will remember, was one of the business partners who owned the building we were leasing and was now also a board member, remarked on live

TV—"Partners, please call and pledge for your new TV station. Our bank account is low and Jim Bakker thinks as long as there are blank checks in the book, he can just keep on writing them!" Jim was not at all amused and left the set hurt and annoyed.

Jim regularly complained to me that I was holding back the progress of TBN—that I should free him up to accelerate the growth and expansion of the ministry. But my pragmatic business sense told me we were heading for financial disaster if Jim was given full rein with no restrictions on him. As a result of the confusion and dissension that followed, God began to lift His blessing from our efforts and also our finances began to suffer.

My children, we learned another important spiritual lesson at this point. Where there is contention and strife, the Holy Spirit is grieved and as a gentle dove, He simply withdraws the blessing and direction of the Lord. I must confess that Jim and I both lost our spiritual direction for a time. One day, in my office, Jim Bakker finally suggested that I leave the ministry. He offered to secure the financing to pay back the gift of $20,000 that Jan and I had given to get the station started.

In the natural, I actually longed to accept his offer and get out while I still had some of my sanity left! But God would not release me, nor could I find any peace in the thought of leaving the ministry that God had so clearly called Jan and me to.

❦

Finally, it got down and dirty! At a board meeting, Jim asked to have several staff members admitted to speak some things that were *"upon their hearts."* I did not know it at the time, but Jim and Tammy had been having regular *"prayer meetings"* with several of the key staff members in their home. What all was prayed about I shall probably never know; but it became clear, as this agonizing board meeting progressed, that Jim had very cleverly and carefully orchestrated a *coup d'état!* The production director, set builder, bookkeeper, and others testified to the board in session that it was Paul Crouch who was holding up the progress of the station and ministry. They recommended my removal and that Jim Bakker be made both president and chairman with full authority to run the operations of the station.

I listened in stunned silence along with the rest of the board as witness after witness—probably about half of the staff—called for my removal.

After the *"kangaroo court"* was ended, Ward Vanguard, the only seasoned businessman on the board, spoke first. Looking directly at me he said, "Paul, you are chairman of this board, and if I were you, I would FIRE Jim Bakker on the spot!"

Jim's face turned pale and his character witnesses all beat a hasty retreat as the other board members unanimously agreed that I should remain in charge of the business affairs of TBN.

Jim's *coup* had failed, but now the strained relationship between Jim and myself became virtually untenable. Division and dissension now reigned throughout the staff—those who supported Jim and those who supported me. We have seen this tragic situation occur again and again in church splits and we always wonder why—why must the Kingdom of God suffer such sorrow and indignity? After nearly seventy years on this earth, I believe I can answer that burning question, and I pray it will guide you and others through similar valleys of despair.

Jim and Tammy, and Jan and I should have called a fast to bring all the staff together, and we should have fallen on our faces before the Lord until we reached unity. God had a perfect plan and solution to our problem—He could have led us through every situation to total unity and victory—but we did not do this. I will always wonder—even thirty years later—if it was not God's perfect plan for Jim Bakker to lead the creative, artistic, and programming wing of the ministry and I, the business and technical wing. Some years later, at a dedication service for Jim's new TV facility back in Charlotte, North Carolina, Jim said to me, "Paul, don't you see it now? God divided us that He might multiply us!"

At the time this sounded right, as TBN and Jim's new PTL Club were both prospering. But now, with all that we know today—seeing the tragic collapse of PTL and Heritage USA—I still wonder if God's first plan was not His best.

Jim and Tammy's private prayer meetings continued with their half of the staff. It finally became clear that Jim was planning an exodus to begin a separate new TV ministry in Southern California. Jan and I felt hopeless, helpless, and depressed. *Where,* we thought, *do we go from here?*

CHAPTER TWELVE

CHANNEL 40—*HALLELUJAH!*

THERE FOLLOWED A TIME IN OUR LIVES SO DARK and filled with such despair that it is painful to even think about it or to recall it in any way. I do not fully understand why those whom we love the most, at times, are the very ones who hurt us the most. I do, however, have a partial answer for you. When at any stage of our lives we are not willing to totally submit our wills to the will of God, I can assure you, trouble will always follow. I have missed God's will more than once, and always lived to regret it. Remember my earlier lesson about finding the will of God? Tragically, neither Jim nor I had allowed that *"PEACE OF GOD"* to *"RULE"* in our hearts.

The only reason I tell you of this time of testing and despair is to let you know that even in the *"valley of the shadow of death,"* our

God is still there! We learned by personal experiences the cry of the psalmist David:

> *Whither shall I go from thy spirit?*
> *or whither shall I flee from thy presence?*
> *If I ascend into heaven, thou art there:*
> *if I make my bed in hell,*
> *behold, thou art there. (Psalm 139:7–8)*

One night in the midst of our pain and despair, the Lord awakened me and it seemed I heard heaven's choir singing that familiar old hymn, "*O LOVE THAT WILL NOT LET ME GO.*" Yes, God does give us songs in the night, and He will not "*suffer you to be tempted above that ye are able; but will with the temptation also make a way to escape, that ye may be able to bear it*" (1 Corinthians 10:13).

I also began to observe an ominous change in my usually bubbly and effervescent sweetheart, Jan. She began to withdraw into a melancholy state, which was strange and frightening to me. For days she would sit in our bedroom without dressing or eating. My boys remember this time most painfully. She has since given her full testimony of this nightmare, which for months none of us could pull her out of. She simply could not function as a wife or a mother. Our boys had to literally learn to cook and wash clothes—we all three had to fend for ourselves as Jan sank ever deeper into complete depression.

In her later testimony she told of how Satan would torment her with visions of herself—locked in some padded cell, rocking and weeping, her mind gone. Finally, the satanic temptation reached the point where she actually planned to walk down to the Pacific Ocean beach, about a mile from our home, and just keep walking—out, out, out, into the cold, dark water. Hopefully everyone would think it was a tragic accident so as not to bring the added shame and sorrow of a suicide upon the family and TBN.

❧

Now the ministry began to falter and stagger even more as Satan hurled attack after attack at the very heart of the ministry.

We have learned that this stripping and emptying process is essential in every life that commits wholly to follow the Lord. We have also learned that it most always occurs just before God begins to thrust a life or a talent into His full service. Months later, Norm Juggert, my fellow TBN board member, put this time of testing into proper perspective. He wrote a note to Jan and me that said in part: *"The Lord has laid it upon my heart to acknowledge the great spiritual growth I have witnessed in your life these past two years. I know, now, that the trials we have experienced were not without purpose. The success of TBN would have provided an almost irresistible inducement for pride, had it not been for the trials that God used to temper and forge character and humility."* Norm has always been a strong source of wise counsel and advice.

The final blow came in August of 1973. The transmitter of Channel 46 up on Mt. Wilson suffered a serious fire in the antenna. We were off the air for several days. When the engineers finally got us back on the air, the picture that was weak and underpowered before was now virtually unviewable. Many parts of Southern California could get neither picture or sound. It looked like the end had finally come.

During all this time we had continued to negotiate with Mr. Myers for the purchase of his TV station, but we were far short of our goal for the large down payment that would be required. Sensing that TBN would not be able to perform under the terms of our preliminary purchase agreement, Mr. Myers began dealing with other potential buyers for the purchase of his station. We finally learned, to our utter devastation and dismay, that a deal had been struck with Ken Connolly, a local pastor, and that within thirty days we would have to give up our programming on the station. Our *"Christian brother"* had literally bought the station out from under us!

I remember walking into my office that next morning with my heart and hopes dashed again! Tears began to flow as I cried out to God for an answer—and again that still, small voice spoke: *"Call Mr. Angel Lerma at Channel 40,"* came the word.

"But Lord," I protested, "I called last summer, that station is not for sale."

God's voice was unmistakable—"CALL!"

☙

I immediately obeyed the Lord and called. To my utter astonishment Mr. Angel Lerma himself answered the phone. I learned later that this was *THE DAY* he had made his decision to sell Channel 40!

The very next morning I was in Mr. Lerma's office in Los Angeles. His mix of Spanish and English programming had not been successful and he was anxious to sell. The price—*one million dollars.* But the good news was—he was willing to finance the bulk of the purchase price with only 10 percent down or $100,000. For once in my life I did not even haggle over the purchase price. This time we signed our purchase agreement in advance of our going on the air. We were much wiser in our business dealings from that time onward.

Just prior to this new opportunity to acquire Channel 40, God had sent Paul and Joyce Toberty into our lives and into our TBN family. Paul was a successful contractor and an international director of the Full Gospel Businessmen's Fellowship. Paul agreed to join our board of directors as vice president. Not only did he and Joyce bring spiritual encouragement, but valuable business experience and financial guarantees as well. In fact, Paul and I, along with our wives, had signed personal guarantees to Mr. Angel Lerma, the seller of Channel 40, pledging to make the $9,044 monthly payments on the station if TBN was ever unable to make them! I remember the strange, almost frightening, feeling as we signed the large, very legal-looking documents. Our lives and now even our homes—in fact, all of our assets were on the line for Christian television.

And yet there was a joy, even an exhilaration—sort of a *"Here we go, Lord; we are in Your hands!"* feeling. We also signed a concurrent airtime contract that permitted us to continue our four hours a day of Christian TV programming on Channel 40 without a break. In fact, we broadcast for several days on both Channel 46 and Channel 40, which gave us the opportunity to tell our partners of the change in channels. Praise God, in only two weeks we were *ON THE AIR on Channel 40* with four times the power and double the population coverage. What seemed to be the greatest tragedy turned out to be one of the greatest blessings of all!

But more trouble loomed on the horizon.

Jim Bakker, realizing the vast new potential of this more powerful Channel 40, made one last attempt to wrest control of the ministry away from Jan and me. For several days, and in countless board sessions, the various members and other spiritual advisors tried vainly to reason with Jim—hoping to yet reach an accommodation for a working relationship between Jim and myself. I was willing to try, but Jim was not. Finally, in anger Jim stalked out of the meeting, cleaned out his desk and office, and left the building without even a word of farewell. In the absence of a written resignation, the board had no choice but to remove him as an officer and director, asking me to serve as the new president of Trinity Broadcasting Network in addition to my duties as chairman of the board.

In a matter of days we learned that Jim had indeed formed a new ministry that he called the Dove Broadcasting Network. About half of the TBN staff had left with Jim and efforts began in earnest to acquire a building and purchase airtime on another TV station. Jan and I were devastated once again to see such dissension and strife as it boiled over into the partners of the ministry, who were now torn as to whom they should support.

Rumors flew thick and fast. We heard that Jim had acquired a large building just a few blocks up the road from TBN and that he was securing time back on Channel 46, which, as I've said, had been purchased by Pastor Kenneth Connolly. But after about two months of their desperate efforts to launch another TV ministry, we learned that Jim and Tammy Bakker had returned to Charlotte, North Carolina, where they did succeed in forming a new TV ministry that became Heritage USA. The rest is well-known history.

One postscript, which I must add to Jim and Tammy's credit, came about a year after they had left Southern California. One afternoon, our home phone rang and it was Jim and Tammy on the other end. Jim said, "Paul and Jan, Tammy and I are calling to say how sorry we are for the way things ended out in California. We feel . . . " Jim's voice paused, as he searched for the right words. "What I'm trying to say is that we feel that God cannot bless us back here in Charlotte because we have held bitterness in our hearts toward you and Jan." Another long pause. "We are calling to ask you to forgive us for anything we may have done to hurt you or the work of TBN."

Jan and I were overjoyed to accept this heartfelt apology and assured them of our unconditional forgiveness. At the same time, we asked them to forgive us for anything we had done to hurt or injure them in any way. We concluded the call in prayer, wishing each other God's best in our future mutual endeavors.

It is interesting to note that soon after that call of reconciliation, both ministries began to prosper in new and unusual ways. May we always remember that God cannot bless and prosper anyone or any ministry where there is bitterness, strife, and unforgiveness. Learn this lesson early in life and it will be one of the important keys to your own success in life.

❧

As things began returning to normal at TBN, a most wonderful healing began in Jan. I remember all too well the long, dark valley she suffered for many months during the horrible birth pangs of TBN. Finally, one Sunday morning, I insisted that she get dressed and go to church with us. I remember even having to help her get up and get ready to go.

As Jan has testified many times, she cannot even remember the service, but at the conclusion she was captivated by a pitiful young girl who had timidly slipped forward at the conclusion of the service and was kneeling all alone at the altar. Suddenly, and for the first time in months, Jan received a word from the Lord— *"You are to go and minister to that young lady."*

"But Lord," she protested, "I am the one who needs to be ministered to!" It seemed that no one even noticed this pitiful soul in tattered clothing and unkempt straggly hair. Finally, the Holy Spirit's urging prevailed, and Jan found herself kneeling beside this stranger who had wandered into First Assembly that Sunday morning. Out of a wounded little soul poured a story of sorrow and abuse that, as Jan said, "made even my trials seem small and insignificant." Tears flowed as confession was made and then the greatest miracle of all, a *NEW BIRTH in Christ!*

You see, without even realizing it at the time, Jan had put into motion another of God's great laws—*you have to give the very thing that you yourself* need*!* (Luke 6:38).

A few nights later I was startled out of my wits as she sat straight up in bed at about 3:00 A.M., *laughing*—yes, *laughing* for the first time in months! The dream tumbled out between laughter and tears—she had been walking, she said, along a seashore. As she walked, she could see in the distance a group of men sitting around a campfire. As she drew closer it was evident from the look of the ancient boats and fishing nets that this was long ago—Bible times!

Finally she saw *HIM!* It was *JESUS*—no doubt about it—so the other men were surely His disciples. As they were talking and eating, someone must have said something very funny and Jesus began to laugh! His laugh was so hearty that He leaned all the way back in an infectious laugh that spread to all the other men. With that—*snap*—Jan was awake two thousand years later, laughing with *none other than Jesus!*

Her healing was complete a short time later when we made our first trip to Israel. As the bus drove along the shore of the beautiful Sea of Galilee, she shouted, "STOP! This is the place—I have been here before!" *Déjà vu—that dream—Jesus and His disciples—* it was there that Jesus healed my Jan, yes, with a divine laugh!

CHAPTER THIRTEEN

THE AGREEMENT IS ILLEGAL

DURING THE EARLY MONTHS OF 1974, GOD'S SPIRIT began moving in a beautiful and spontaneous new way. Phone calls increased dramatically as hundreds called to accept Christ as Savior—*on LIVE TV!* Word of this new television ministry began to spread like wildfire all across Southern California. Wonder of wonders, God was doing an exciting *NEW* thing through a media that had heretofore been dominated by the world—*television!*

Melodyland Christian Center and Pastor Ralph Wilkerson had helped us through these early stages of development with much-needed TV cameras and other equipment. While Ralph and I had strong philosophical disagreement on the future and direction of TBN, I will ever be grateful for his vision in assisting us during these early pioneering efforts. The problem was: He who has the cameras makes the rules. If we made decisions (particularly in programming) that were in agreement with Pastor Ralph, the cameras stayed—if we didn't, it seemed the cameras were needed at the church. Several nights we were simply off the air because the cameras were gone!

Pastor Jerry Barnard of San Diego recalled at least one wild goose chase, driving the ninety miles up to Santa Ana, only to be told that cameras had been pulled at the last minute—and we were off the air! Occasionally, ONE CAMERA would be left—a small, home-quality Sony, which forced us to create some rather innovative new production techniques!

My boys should remember at least one night in particular. Paul Jr. was the director, and Matt operated the camera with the help of a box to make him tall enough! The trick was getting from the interview set over to the singers without a switcher. The problem was solved with a simple black card. When the host introduced the music, the card was placed over the lens of the camera. Quickly, the camera panned over to the music set and the black card was removed—*presto*—music and all without a glitch!

Pastor Ralph Wilkerson became increasingly unhappy as his efforts to move the entire TV operations to his church met with continued opposition from the board, and myself in particular.

❧

Finally, without any real explanation for his request, Ralph urged that Ward Vanguard be removed from the board of directors. I was devastated, since Ward had been my staunch supporter throughout the whole Jim Bakker affair and had also voted to keep TBN independent of any one church, which I knew was mandatory if we were to serve all of the churches and Body of Christ. At the time, I could only conclude that this move was to gain more control of the board of directors. I tried to reason with Ralph, but he was adamant—Ward had to go—he insisted that I call a meeting of the board to remove him!

When I broke the news to Ward, he was incensed. He reminded me of the considerable investment of time, and even finances, that he had placed in TBN during the first year of operations. After all, he and his business partners had furnished the building and studio that we were beaming the program from—and did I remember they had given us the first three months rent-free?

I sympathized and agreed, but I reminded Ward that we were held virtually hostage to Melodyland Christian Center for the use of their cameras. Ward fumed that the church was being amply compensated by the free airtime they were receiving for their church program, as well as the exposure they received each time Ralph hosted the *Praise the Lord* program.

Finally, Ward Vanguard looked at me with eyes flashing and said, "Paul, I have no quarrel with you, but if Ralph insists on removing me from the board of TBN, I will have no recourse but to sue him and TBN!"

Fear filled my heart at these words, and I pled with Ward to reconsider. I reminded him that TBN was still in its infancy—that litigation would probably sink us! We had no resources—how would we even be able to afford to pay for legal defense? All reasoning was fruitless—Ward was furious. His parting words were "I'll see you and Ralph in court!"

Once again, I was devastated. With all the other problems and agonies we had endured, how would we handle this one? A few days later, and to my surprise, Ward tendered his resignation rather than be removed from the board, but still vowed to see us all in court! It was Friday as I drove home to break the news of our latest impending disaster to Jan.

The next day, an urgent call came through to our home—"Ward Vanguard has been rushed to Hoag Hospital in Newport Beach—he is in intensive care—please pray!" The following day, which was Sunday, was the first day visitors were even permitted. The doctor said I could only stay a few minutes. He also confided that the illness was a mystery—they couldn't seem to even diagnose what the problem was.

As I entered the intensive care room, I was shocked and saddened. Machines and tubes were connected to Ward, it seemed, everywhere. A respirator was breathing for him—he was totally unconscious and probably unaware of my presence. All I could do was offer a brief prayer before being ushered out of the room. I learned, to my sorrow and dismay, that Ward Vanguard, my faithful supporter and friend, had passed away early Monday morning.

With heavy heart, all I could do was to commit this devastating circumstance and my brother Ward Vanguard to the Lord.

❦

This was the summer of 1974, and we had finally completed and filed our application with the Federal Communications Commission for the purchase of Channel 40. Now came the agonizing wait to see if our application would be approved. We had been on the air for almost one year now; purchasing time first on Channel 46 and now on Channel 40. We were finally on the homestretch—we would know in about ninety days if God's people would finally OWN their very own 100-percent-Christian TV station.

Ralph Wilkerson knew that the continued assistance of his church was essential since we were, as yet, unable to purchase TV cameras and equipment of our own. So, as a final condition for that equipment assistance, Ralph asked that at a minimum, his church board be given absolute control over the board of TBN.

With Jim Bakker gone and Ward Vanguard dead, the board of TBN was down to Ralph Wilkerson, Paul Toberty, Norm Juggert, and me. Paul, Norm, and I were all in agreement that this was not the right decision, but what could we do? Cameras cost $50,000 each, not to mention the many other pieces of equipment necessary to produce TV programs. We searched and called everywhere, but to no avail. Finally, with no alternative, we agreed to Ralph's conditions.

For three days, four attorneys and two certified public accountants, along with the combined boards of directors of Melodyland and TBN, hammered out the contracts. TBN would remain a separate corporation, but the Melodyland board, which Ralph was chairman of, would have veto power and control over all the affairs of TBN. I remember the uneasy feeling in the pit of my stomach as I, along with the rest of the TBN board, signed the voluminous, multisectioned contract.

The ink had hardly dried on the documents when it became all too apparent that our new "partners" had very different goals and ideas for the direction of TBN. Demands and directives were issued that came into direct conflict with the many promises we had made to the partners and supporters of TBN. Jan and I found ourselves in another bitter struggle for TBN's independence.

God taught me one of the bitterest lessons of all in this college of "hard knocks." Day after day, and night after night, we agonized in prayer. There were times when I could not pray. The heavens were brass—God seemed so far away. We tried to extract ourselves from this agreement we had signed in return for equipment and technical assistance, but it had been drawn up by four top attorneys and two CPAs—*we had sold our birthright!* In addition to the agony of losing our position and ministry, we felt as though we had failed God and the partners who had worked so hard with us to bring it thus far. The blackness and bitterness were more than we could bear.

A few days later my phone rang. Norm Juggert, my fellow TBN board member and attorney, was on the other end. "Paul," he said, "I just may have some good news for you."

My heart leaped for the millionth time!

"The agreement we all signed with Melodyland . . ." He paused for a moment. "I think it may be invalid because it seems to be in conflict with certain provisions of the California Corporations Code . . . what I mean is, I believe the whole agreement is illegal."

For several moments I was speechless—could this be the release we had prayed for so earnestly?

"I need to do some more research on this to be certain," Norm continued. "I'll be in touch with you shortly."

❦

As I hung up the phone my mind was in a whirl. Suddenly, a memory flashback exploded in my mind. I remembered a strange encounter I had experienced on the very day we had signed this fateful agreement. Back in my office an unusual lady had asked to see me in private. She was elegantly dressed, in her early to middle fifties; but there was something very different in her appearance and mannerism. She had a most penetrating look—and she seemed to be able to see into my very soul! I had never met this woman before, but she knew my name.

"Paul," she said sternly, "I have a message for you from the Lord." As she spoke she opened her Bible and read from a passage in Isaiah 28.

> *You have made a covenant with death . . . but your*
> *covenant . . . shall be cancelled and your agreement . . .*
> *shall not stand.*

With hardly another word she closed her Bible, stood up, and left my office. In thirty years, I have not seen or heard from this woman again.

I remembered how strange and uneasy I had felt—*"Dear God,"* I thought, *"even if this message is from You, what can I do now?"* The agreement was signed, sealed, and delivered.

The memory of this meeting and my strange visitor passed like a flash through my mind as Norm's final words rang in my ears—"The whole agreement is illegal." A few days later, Norm's research confirmed the fact that our agreement was, indeed, illegal! God had blinded the eyes of four attorneys, two CPAs, plus the combined boards of Melodyland and TBN, to the illegality of this agreement that was not God's will for *HIS* TV station. *We were free!* Free to keep our promise that Channel 40 would ever and always belong to all of God's people; free to allow all the ministries and churches to be a part; free to depend on God alone.

Yes, God taught me one of the bitterest lessons of all and chastened me most severely. By His grace and love, I have learned that lesson well.

The next Sunday night at First Assembly, where God had earlier and so beautifully confirmed our divine call, God gave us yet another powerful confirmation that we were back on track, and that He was moving us ever closer to the great purpose for our lives. Jan's *Living Bible* fell open to 2 Corinthians 8:10–11, which read:

> *I want to suggest that you finish what you started to do a year ago, for you were not only the first to propose this idea, but the first to begin doing something about it. Having started the ball rolling so enthusiastically, you should carry this project through to completion just as gladly, giving whatever you can out of whatever you have. Let your enthusiastic idea at the start be equalled by your realistic action now.*

It was Sunday, April 21, 1974, when God gave us this wonderful word of encouragement. When Jan checked our diary later that night, it was exactly *ONE YEAR TO THE DAY* that we had first walked into the studio of what would become TBN! We laughed and cried again, praising the Lord for this message of His faithfulness and love.

CHAPTER FOURTEEN

A $35,000 LUTHERAN

BUT NOW, AS A RESULT OF OUR INVALID AGREE-MENT with Melodyland Christian Center, Pastor Ralph withdrew all equipment assistance and also asked to be released as guarantor on a lease of $137,000 for some TV equipment that TBN had been able to secure in its own name. Further, and to our surprise, a phone call came from one of the board members at Faith Center, the owners of Channel 30 TV. The board member advised me that Pastor Ralph was attempting to purchase Channel 30, which was now experiencing some financial difficulties.

When I called James Gammon, our FCC attorney in Washington, with this news, he was extremely concerned. It was obvious that Ralph was unaware of FCC rules at that time, which prohibited ownership in more than one station in the same market.

"Ralph must resign from the board of TBN immediately," he declared. Also, and most serious of all, Jim said, "It could deny the grant of your application for Channel 40 at the FCC!"

With that, I immediately called a board meeting that Ralph did not attend, even though he was given proper notice. The board of TBN did the only thing it could do—we removed him from the board, lest there be even the hint of a cloud upon our FCC application for the license of Channel 40, which was now nearing a decision by the FCC in Washington.

Ralph said later that we had acted improperly and sought a reversal of this action by the board of TBN, but our action was both legally necessary and final. We were at last free of outside control. Now the board of TBN was down to three: Norm Juggert, Paul Toberty, and myself. But we were also free of any financial guarantor as we approached a most important deadline for the purchase of Channel 40. One of the main qualifications for any FCC application is that of financial ability to both purchase and operate a TV station. You will recall that we had agreed to make a $100,000 down payment to Mr. Angel Lerma, the owner, and that he had agreed to finance the balance of the $1,000,000 purchase price over the next eight years.

We had worked very hard during the early months of 1974 to raise the $100,000. We had held several minithons and spoken of the need each night on the *Praise the Lord* program. We had contacted foundations and had called every "rich uncle" we could think of from coast to coast! As I have mused so often when telling this story—all we got that month was the largest telephone bill we had ever received!

Finally, things got desperate—we had a firm deadline to place our $100,000 down payment into the escrow account of our bank. That day had finally arrived! We had been successful in raising $65,000 toward the down payment, but were far short of our goal. We learned later that there were actually three other parties that had offered Mr. Lerma more money for his station and were hoping that we would default! Not only would we lose the purchase agreement and the whole station, but even our $65,000 would be forfeited under the terms of the agreement! Once again, it seemed that all was lost!

My children, another great lesson was about to be learned. I have since asked the Lord why, it seems, that He always waits to the very last minute to deliver us. Why must we always be at the bank of the *"Red Sea"* with the *"Egyptians"* swooping down on our backsides with no way of escape? The answer came later in my quiet time of prayer as I sincerely asked the Lord for an answer. He said, *"Son, it is so that when the victory comes—there is never any doubt who did it!"*

Yes, these times of extreme testing are absolutely necessary, for without them, our flesh would be tempted to take the credit, pride would follow, and then what does the Word say about that? *"PRIDE GOETH BEFORE DESTRUCTION"* (Proverbs 16:18).

No, I don't like these heart-seizure kinds of tests any more than you do and, by the way, we have all had them; but they are absolutely essential to our spiritual growth and maturity. By the way, they will get worse and even more frequent as you move deeper into spiritual warfare! But ah—the *VICTORIES*, the *VICTORIES!*

I shall never forget *THAT DAY*—a day that shall be enshrined in the history of TBN as one of the greatest miracles of all!

The mail that day was dismal—we received only a fraction of what was needed. The typical daily financial report from my secretary was as follows:

> *Paul: Unless the Lord performs a miracle, we will not have a payday on Friday. We are in the red ($371.64). I have held the following checks: Baker Equipment Rental, $103.91; A-1 Janitor Supply, $131.83; and Orange Coast Hardware, $261.88.*
>
> *P.S. However, today's deposit is $246.63.*

Jan was in the prayer chapel crying out to the Lord in tears—eyelashes gone, mascara streaking her cheeks! I was praying and pacing back and forth in my office—by now it was about 2:30 and the bank *closed* at 3:00! Some of the staff members were cleaning out their desks—this was it—great while it lasted, but now it was time to go find a real job!

Suddenly my phone rang. My secretary said, "Paul, there is a strange little man out here asking to see you." "SEND HIM IN!" I shouted. "SEND ANYONE IN THAT COMES FROM NOW ON!" I added.

This time our miracle appeared in the form of a *Lutheran* brother: *Scotty Scotvold!* I have told this story many times, but I want it recorded so you don't forget it! You see, there was not only a great miracle here, but another important lesson that I had to learn. As I have said so often, if I were God, I would not have chosen a Lutheran! *Lutherans weren't even Pentecostal, were they?* Surely God should have chosen an Assemblies of God brother—even Church of God—I would have settled for Pentecostal Holiness, although we didn't agree 100 percent with them either, especially since *"eyelashes"* are forbidden!

Oh, how deeply rooted, our little pet traditions and doctrines. How unaware of these silly prejudices most of us are. God wanted me to know that HIS BODY was a lot bigger than I had imagined it to be! He wanted me to know that TBN was to be a *bridge builder—a repairer of the breach—a healing balm within His church.* How hard do these lifelong prejudices die—these traditions so carefully taught within the many denominational factions called Christian! I can testify to you all that most of those hateful, hurtful divisions died within me as this slight-of-stature stranger stood before me that day.

Finally he spoke: "Paul," he said, "I have been so blessed by your TV programs, and for God's people to have their very own TV station is almost too good to be true."

I was wishing he would hurry because it was now about 2:45—the bank closed in fifteen minutes!

Scotty continued, "I was on my way to buy a yacht when God spoke to me."

What, does God speak to Lutherans? I thought. My prejudices were beginning to die, but they were not dead yet.

With that he reached into his coat pocket and with trembling hand, held out a folded piece of paper that appeared to be—*could it be—A CHECK?*

My heart was bursting as I quickly unfolded it—*yes, a check and as God is my witness, it was exactly* $35,000! My eyes filled with tears as I literally raced for the door! I'm sure at the time, Scotty must have wondered if I had lost my senses! I didn't even say thank you—*it was now ten minutes until 3:00!* Up the street I flew, breaking every speed law in this race with time.

Fortunately, our bank was not far, but I distinctly remember looking at the clock as I burst through the doors of United California Bank of Santa Ana—it was *five minutes until 3:00!* I rushed to the escrow office and triumphantly laid the check on the officer's desk, directing that it be dated and placed immediately into our Channel 40 escrow account.

I also called Angel Lerma, the owner, to let him know his $100,000 down payment was IN THE BANK!

When I returned to my office Scotty was gone, but Jan and the staff were rejoicing! Later, of course, over and over with tears I thanked precious Scotty Scotvold, my *NEW LUTHERAN BROTHER,* for hearing God's voice, but even more important, for obeying God's voice that had literally, and at the very last moment, saved Channel 40 for all of God's people. *Praise the Lord—the pillar of cloud and fire were still leading His simple, little children!* Our joy overflowed that night on the *Praise the Lord* program as we told of God's miraculous intervention once again to save HIS TV station and ministry.

As of this writing, Scotty and his dear wife, Lucille, are still faithful partners of TBN, which has grown from one station to over 4,000 TV stations and is still growing! Scotty—the Body of Christ honors you for your selfless obedience to the voice of God.

You know—I never did ask if he ever got his yacht!

CHAPTER FIFTEEN

$137,000 IN BAD CHECKS

FOR DAYS, THE EUPHORIA OF OUR GREAT MIRACLE lingered. But one great final hurdle remained before we would see the final victory and before we would finally claim the TV station that it seemed we had already given our life's blood for. We had leased $137,000 worth of TV equipment with which we were producing the *Praise the Lord* program, plus a few other programs that we were still purchasing time for on Channel 40. Melodyland Christian Center and Pastor Ralph Wilkerson had asked to be released from the financial guarantee that they had provided on this lease, as I have already explained.

Even though Pastor Wilkerson and I had very strong differences on the future of Christian TV, and those differences boiled over into many areas of the Body of Christ, the final chapter of our relationship with Melodyland and Pastor Ralph does have a happy ending. Parenthetically, my sons Paul Jr. and Matt, will remember the many intense discussions Jan and I had concerning our relationship and struggle with Pastor Ralph over the control and direction of TBN. Matt, you may remember the day our family was driving down the freeway—I think we had just come from one of our traumatic meetings with Pastor Ralph. Your mother and I, as usual, were discussing the sorry state of affairs between Melodyland and TBN. Of course, the central theme was Pastor Ralph and his various directives and demands for the future of TBN. It was always: "Ralph this" or "Ralph that." Finally, you, Matt, about twelve years old at the time, raised up out of the backseat of our car where you had been playing with your brother, Paul Jr., and exclaimed, *"RALPH, RALPH, RALPH—all I ever hear is RALPH! Can't we ever talk about ANYTHING but RALPH?"*

Yes, sometimes out of the mouth of babes comes wisdom! Your mother and I were racked with laughter and at the same time rebuked by your youthful but penetrating wisdom that had, no doubt, come from the Holy Spirit Himself! I'm sure that if Jan and I, along with Ralph, had listened more closely to the voice of the Holy Spirit, we would have not had those traumatic encounters that I have detailed for you in this account.

Well, since Melodyland had asked to be removed as guarantors on the lease, the leasing company as well as the FCC had to have some new proof that TBN could make it on its own. The payoff, as I have told you, was $137,000, and we simply didn't have it; nor did we have another guarantor to cosign with us. Jan and I had exhausted everything we had just to complete the down payment of $100,000. We seemed to be at a total impasse once again.

Paul Toberty and I had shopped all over Southern California, trying to get new leases, even trying to get our current leasing company to rewrite them for TBN. But in 1974 money was tight—TBN was new. We did not have a "track record," they said. They could not be sure that TBN could make the payments without a financial guarantor. Without a guarantor they would have to repossess the TV equipment! We were desperate once more!

Finally one afternoon, as Paul Toberty and I sat staring at each other in my office, a new light that I had not seen before flashed in Paul's eyes. "Let's write the checks," he said.

For a moment it did not even dawn on me what he meant. "Write what checks?" I asked.

"The equipment lease payoff checks," Paul replied.

You mean the whole $137,000?" I asked.

"Yes, let's write them by faith," was Paul's firm reply.

There was a long pause as the possibility of it all sank in on me. "All right, call Harold, the bookkeeper," I replied.

The whole idea was crazy to Harold. "All I know is you'll be writing $137,000 in bad checks," he laughed. Nevertheless, the order was given and the checks were written. Paul and I called our small staff together that afternoon as we laid the checks on the altar before the Lord in our little prayer chapel. We joined hearts and hands as we cried out to God for yet another miracle. *But, now what?* You can't cash checks without the actual funds on deposit to back them up.

❦

As I drove home that afternoon, the Lord once more spoke to my spirit. *"Whose station is Channel 40?"* the Lord asked.

"Yours and the people's," I replied.

The Lord spoke again, *"Who has always helped you when you had a need?"*

My answer came immediately. "Your people, Lord." By the time I reached home, the light of God's revelation was shining in my eyes and Jan knew something new was up! "We're going to have a Praise-a-Thon tonight!" I exclaimed.

Jan and the Tobertys were all negative to the idea. "We just had our spring Praise-a-Thon two months ago—it is too soon," they said. But I knew that God had spoken. In fact I had seen, as it were, a vision as to just how we were to begin. I saw us all kneeling on the *Praise the Lord* set, humbling ourselves before God and man on live television!

By now, Jan and I were back at the TV studio getting ready for the regular *Praise the Lord* program. We conferred with the Tobertys by phone. They shared a Scripture in Exodus that they felt the Lord was quickening to them. The consensus seemed to be that we should "stand still, and see the salvation of the Lord" (Exodus 14:13). But as we read the Scripture together again, one verse exploded before us!

*THE LORD SAID TO MOSES, "QUIT PRAYING
AND GET THE PEOPLE MOVING! FORWARD,
MARCH!" (Exodus 14:15 TLB)*

"We'll be there as soon as we can," the Tobertys said. "Go
ahead and get the Praise-a-Thon started!"

I am sure that the world, anyone who happened to tune in
Channel 40 that night, wondered what peculiar people these were,
kneeling on LIVE TV, confessing to their God that they were helpless without Him—that they needed a miracle once again.

I once said to Jan, "If I ever do write a book, I think I should
title it *AND THE PHONES RANG, AND RANG, AND RANG."*
Yes, every time we had a crisis—every time we were at the *"Red
Sea,"* it was *GOD'S WONDERFUL PEOPLE* on the phone,
again saying, "Go for it, Paul and Jan—we are with you!"

This night was no different. *"Ten dollars from Covina . . . fifteen
dollars from Sylmar . . . one hundred dollars from Los Angeles . . .
twenty-five dollars from Tehachapi . . ."* as Jan read the pledges.
The checks which we had written by faith lay on the table before
us as God began the heavenly deposit through His beautiful
people. By the end of that first night, well over $40,000 had been
pledged! Praise God, the heavenly manna was falling!

But our faith was to be tested once again. On the next night,
we received a very special call. The man said he was a Christian
dentist and a partner of TBN. He gave his name and a pledge of

$1,000! In those early days, this was an enormous pledge! He challenged other dentists and doctors to call and match his pledge.

Again, the phones began to ring. The dentists were responding—up and up went the pledges! Now the doctors were calling, too. A $3,000 pledge from one; $5,000 from another. Our total was nearing our goal of $137,000. Finally our dentist *"partner"* called back and said, "STOP THE TELETHON." He said he would meet with us next Sunday for dinner and would bring a check to complete our goal of $137,000! But something did not witness with our spirits. The Holy Spirit, through His gift of a word of knowledge, was warning us—we DID NOT STOP the Praise-a-Thon.

The next day, as we phoned to verify the pledges, we were devastated. Most of the larger ones were phony. We had been deceived to the tune of many thousands of dollars. Now what? How would we explain and tell the real partners of this treachery? We prayed for wisdom and strength. I knew we had to be completely open and transparent with our partners, so tearfully the next night we told the whole, sad story. We moved our total board back; but now it was God's move once again.

❧

The phones were silent as Jan and I poured out our hearts and told of how we had been so cruelly deceived—of how our spirits had been troubled and warned by the Holy Spirit. But now, once again, the phones began to ring! And they rang and rang once more. Before the evening was over, God's true sons and daughters from all over Southern California had replaced the phony pledges with true pledges. We were back on track, moving toward the final phase of God's great miracle for HIS TV station that, for the first time, would cover the whole of Southern California—over twelve million souls who would soon have 100-percent-Christian television.

We had begun the Praise-a-Thon on Thursday, and by Monday we had reached our goal of $137,000. I called our attorney, Mr. James Gammon, in Washington to tell him the good news. He relayed the message to the FCC, which moved our application into the final phase.

Thousands of God's people rejoiced with us! We had passed our final hurdle—the *promised land* was finally in view. We now knew we were on the homestretch for the license of Channel 40—God's people were about to claim *THEIR VERY OWN 100-percent-Christian TV station.*

But as God would have it, I received the news not in Santa Ana, but in Chicago. I had traveled to the offices of the German-made Ferenseh camera company to check out their latest equipment. In the middle of intense negotiations for new TV cameras, I was interrupted with this message—*"Have Paul Crouch call Mr. James Gammon in Washington—it is urgent!"*

COMMISSION GRANTED!

WE HAD FILED OUR APPLICATION FOR THE LICENSE of Channel 40 in early May. Knowing that it took the FCC about ninety days to process a fairly routine application, we knew that decision time was near. This application may have been routine for the Commission, but it surely was NOT for us! We had sweated blood and come through hell and high water to see THIS APPLICATION to its final stage.

When the call came to me there in Chicago, I knew it had to be about our application since it came from our FCC attorney; but I also knew the decision could be DENIED just as well as GRANTED! I asked the camera salesman if I could please use his telephone. As I dialed the number, my heart was racing! I had to sit down—cold sweat broke out on my forehead. I'm sure

western union

Telegram

SAA225(1659)(1-03687IC214002)PD 08/02/74 1656
TLX WU RB BCH WSH
ZCZC 002 (COLLECT) RBWASHINGTON DC 08-02 448P EDT
PMS TRINITY BROADCASTING NETWORK INC
111 WEST DYER RD
SANTAANA CA
COMMISSION GRANTED BTC-7389 VOLUNTARY TRANSFER OF CONTROL OF LICENSE
CORPORATION TO TRINITY BROADCASTING NETWORK, INC. NECESSARY C.N-
SUMMATE WITHIN FORTY-FIVE DAYS. NOTIFY COMMISSION UPON CONSUMMATION
AND REMIT GRANT FEE OF TWENTY FIVE THOUSAND THREE HUNDRED TWENTY-
EIGHT DOLLARS IMMEDIATELY THEREAFTER
   WALLACE E JOHNSON CHIEF BROADCAST BUREAU FEDERAL COMMU..ICATIUNS
   COMMISSION
NNNN

ugust 2, 1974, the FCC telegram finally came! I picked it up personally as
e claimed our first TV station, Channel 40, in Southern California.

Behind the Scenes—our second longest running TBN program! The small table was part of our home bedroom set.

1973—our first *Family Christmas TV Special.* The set was mostly compose of the Christmas cards from our wonderful pioneer partners.

aul Jr. recording progress on our new **TBN studio** that we built in Tustin, California. Thirty years later he still has a camera on his shoulder—occasionally!

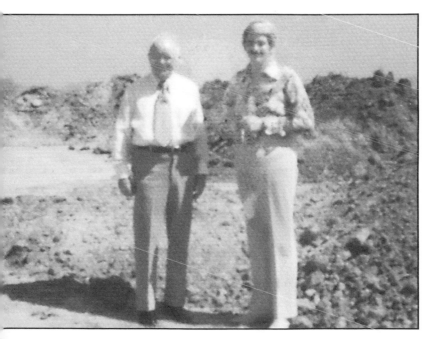

apa Bethany (Jan's dad) and I as we walked and prayed over the new TBN tudio site. He would say, "Children, put on your **FAITH GLASSES!**"

April 10, 1978, our mighty new **satellite station** flashed ON THE AIR! We anointed it with Holy Land oil as hundreds of our pioneer partners helped dedicate it to the Lord! The first 100% Christian satellite station in the world! *"And I saw another angel . . . "* (Rev. 14:6).

This picture, taken as the satellite station was under construction, surprised us all! This *light from the heavens* is still a mystery!

1 1992 Hughes Galaxy let me put a **microchip Bible** on board the new
atellite—G-V. As of this writing, it is still up there beaming TBN 24-hours a
ay! I placed a second Bible on its new replacement scheduled to blast off in
003.

CBI—our pioneer radio station at **Central Bible College** in Springfield,
Iissouri. With fifty whole watts we signed her on with all the pomp and
rcumstance of NBC! The first words—**"HELLO WORLD!"**

The Oval Office—it's pretty clear the President is more interested in the camera than me!

The day we met **Queen Elizabeth II** and **Prince Philip** on the Caribbean island of Nevis. I spoke to her briefly about TBN's first foreign TV station just across the road from the Governor General's house. It seems I am still looking at the station!

We were honored to meet **Pope John Paul II** in Rome and speak to him briefly (real briefly) about TBN's stations in Italy. With me was **Norm Juggert,** our TBN secretary and attorney, and my son **Matthew.**

We presented a Proclamation for Peace to **Menachem Begin** signed by over million TBN partners. We met with **Yasser Arafat** and gave the Palestinians their first TV station in Ramallah in exchange for some TBN programming. Sadly, peace is still very elusive in the land of the Bible—but someday . . . !

President Violeta de Chamorro of Nicaragua, with **Jonas Gonzales Sr.,
Laurie** (Matt's wife), Jan and me. She gave us a TV license the same day,
probably because of **Caylan** who won her heart!

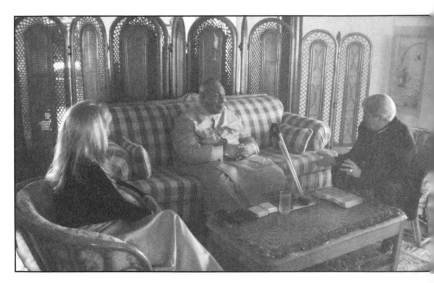

King Taufa'ahau Tupou of Tonga. He not only gave us a TV station for his
South Pacific nation, but helped us dedicate it by throwing the sign-on switch

President Arnoldo Alemán of Nicaragua as we met with him for prayer, and to deliver emergency aid following the devastation of Hurricane Mitch.

President Carlos Flores of Honduras as we prayed for and delivered relief goods after Hurricane Mitch.

President Emil Constantinescu of Romania opened the door to TBN for his nation.

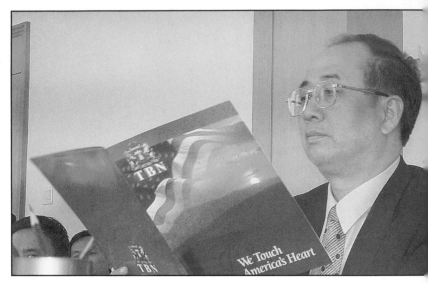

Chinese Minister of Information, **Zhao Qizheng**, was fascinated by the concept of an all Christian TV network. His ministry is an important key to TBN in all of the People's Republic of China. Keep praying!

Vice Premier Qian Qichen of the PRC welcomed us to the largest nation on earth! We are reaching part of China, but will not rest until all billion-plus souls can hear the good news!

House Speaker **Newt Gingrich** pledged his support to a new law to protect our TV licenses. Thank God, it passed!

PRC Minister of Information agreed in principle to TBN in China.

Dr. Elizabeth Vaughn joined me in meeting Chinese officials. Dr. Vaughn has opened the door with her gift of free eye treatment to many in China.

Old friends meet in Washington, D.C. **John Ashcroft** and I grew up together in Springfield, Missouri. We both attended Central Assembly of God Church. Oh, yes, he is now Attorney General of the USA!

Nelson Mandela assured me that TBN would be welcome in South Africa under his administration as president. That promise paid off as later problem developed! We are still on the air! PTL!

wo of the dearest friends in the history of TBN. **Roy Rogers** and **Dale vans** gave us many "Happy Trails" through the years. Their "Long Winding oads" have, indeed, "turned to GOLD"!

Jan and I have had the joy and honor of greeting **Dr. Billy Graham** many times through the years. He is, indeed, the Christian champion of our generation. His classic evangelistic crusades still air on TBN, leading even more to Christ!

Trinity Music City (TMC) USA brought Nashville/Hendersonville into the TBN family. Formerly "Twitty City," home to country music superstar Conway Twitty, it now sends "Praise the Lord" around the world every week

Jan and the program department have used the great "church auditorium" of TMC to produce great dramas, TV specials, and "Praise the Lord" for all of us at TBN and the world.

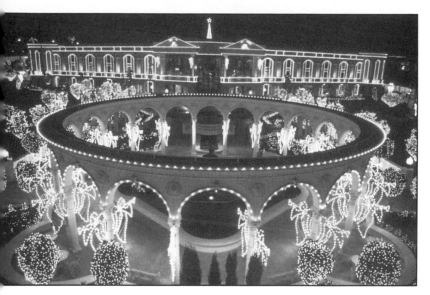

Trinity Christian City International (TCCI), the newest home for TBN headquarters in Costa Mesa, California. Jan's lights and angels are a holiday treat and have caused many to check out TBN-TV!

Jan and I had the joy of cutting the welcome ribbon to TCCI as we dedicated it to the Lord. Built by the Full Gospel Businessmen in 1980, TBN acquired it in 1996. When we dedicated it, Richard Shakarian said, "My father, Demos, built this; but it took Jan to decorate it!"

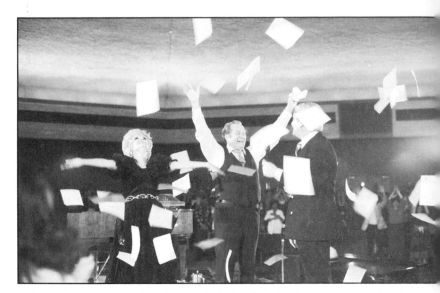

What a night in Phoenix—hundreds had called in for salvation as **R.W. Schambach** preached a classic sermon. I couldn't help it—I threw hundreds of white salvation slips into the air in ecstasy as partners from coast-to-coast praised the Lord!

A few nights after **9-11-01**, we called a nationwide prayer meeting to remember our American heroes and to pray for the thousands of suffering and bereaved. We continue to pray for our President and all in authority. Oh, yes—God bless our beloved America!

God bless our great President Ronald Reagan for proclaiming 1983—"The Year of the Bible." Dr. Bill Bright served as National Chairman, and all of us on the committee had the honor of signing along with the President. Enemies filed suit to try and stop it, but before the courts could act the year was over. Ha, ha devil!

Dr. Robert Cooke, Chairman of the National Religious Broadcasters, along with **Ben Armstrong** and many from America and South Africa, helped dedicate the first Christian TV station in South Africa. TBN Ciskei-East London is still on the air, and now satellite covers the whole continent of Africa. Praise the Lord!

I was overjoyed as our Jerusalem guide and driver invited me to visit his apartment in East Jerusalem. There, to my amazement, were his two children watching "Kids Club" live from America on "Hot Bird" satellite covering Europe and the Middle East.

DBS—"Devil Bustin' Satellite," came on the air in 1995. I had a lot of fun with this announcement— "I'm in love with a new dish!" This new satellite technology has brought TBN to over 18 million new homes through Echostar and DirecTV! They had to pry that dish from my embrace!

Paul Jr. learned filmmaking young, just like his younger
brother Matthew. Paul served as second-unit director on
"Omega Code" and "Megiddo." Wow—what a team!

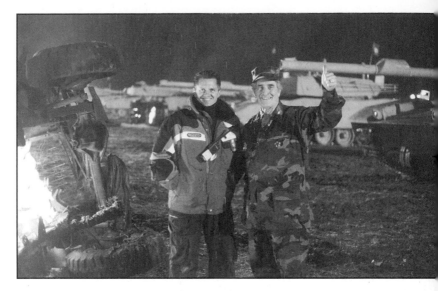

I joined Matthew and had fun hamming it up as we filmed the "Battle of Armageddon" scene for "Megiddo." What a night—we nearly froze to death!

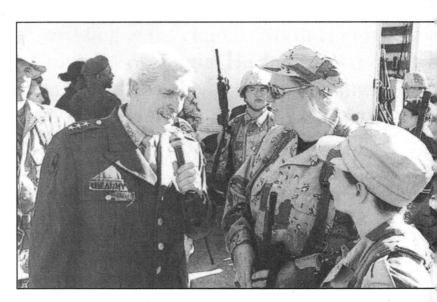

"General" Crouch thanked dozens of brave TBN volunteers who gave of their time to film "Megiddo." Some were in the actual U.S. military which brought even greater realism to the screen. God bless them!

Cameras and filmmaking were "in the blood"! Matthew borrowed my 8mm camera for a school class project. The grade? . . . **A**, of course! Little did we realize that 25 years later, "Omega Code" would make the top ten theatrical release nationwide! And, yes, he's still making movies. "Carman the Champion" and "Megiddo" were next—with more to come, I'm sure!

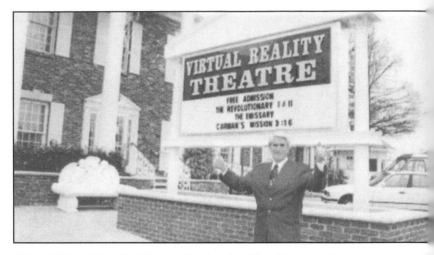

Three "Virtual Reality Theaters" bring the life of Jesus to the screen in breathtaking high definition reality. We have added the life of the Apostle Paul, "Omega Code," and "Megiddo." A fourth theater is coming to Miami.

I was too young for WWII and too old for Korea and Viet Nam, so "Megiddo" helped fulfill a childhood fantasy of going to war. My hero was General George Patton, of course. These brave TBN volunteers actually saluted me! "Megiddo" is still winning souls for the army of the Lord!

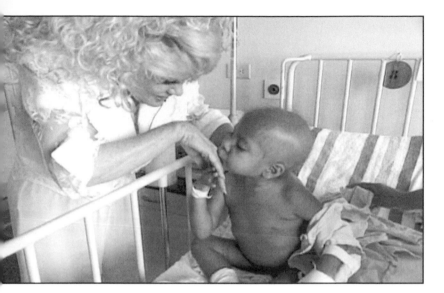

One of Jan's favorite pictures—a little angel going through chemotherapy for cancer—kissing Jan's hand in thanks for a toy doll with hair!

A South African orphanage made up a song to sing to Jan—"The Lady that Brought the Toys."

One of twins from Ethiopia thank Jan for toys.

This is "Sarah from Haiti."

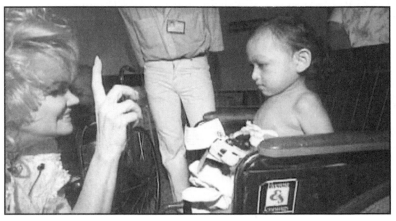
A precious Arab child in Jerusalem hearing about Jesus who sent the gift.

My father's mother, **Agnes Leaming Crouch**. To me there has been no greater saint of God. *Those eyes . . . those eyes.*

My mother and father—**Andrew Franklin** and **Sarah Matilda Crouch**.

My father, Andrew Crouch, in Egypt being carried as we boarded ship for home in 1939. His heart had become so weakened, the doctor ordered him not to climb stairs.

My German nurse, **Heidi Hanover,** with me at age seven shortly before my father died. While in America, she accepted Jesus as her Savior. Back home in Germany she led many to Christ during WWII.

Our "BIG DAY"—August 25, 1957. Papa Bethany honored us with a classic wedding at his church, North Highland Assembly in Columbus, Georgia. He and Jan's mother, **Laurie Elizabeth**, are at the left. To the right is my mother, Sarah Matilda, and my brother-in-law and best man, **Bernard Ridings**.

On August 25, 1985, Jan and I celebrated our son Matthew's marriage to Laurie Orndorff at Crystal Cathedral. Yes, 45 years later, we are still sweethearts!

How we wish we could have kept you both like this forever! **Matt,** we finally broke you from sucking your thumb—by bribery! **Paul Jr.** was his baby brother's best protector ever!

Matthew actually proposed to Laurie on LIVE TV! I think you knew pretty much what her answer would be.

Shiloh Ranch in Colleyville, Texas. The horses were gifts from dear partners. Prince, on the left, and Miss Sunday, who was born on the ranch one Sunday!

My pride and joy, **"Prince"**— a pure white Arabian stallion. Prince has since gone to heaven and is waiting to carry me next to Jesus at the "Second Coming." Dave Lane, our partner in Tennessee, gave me a new white Arabian who is at Trinity Music City in Hendersonville, Tennessee. Come see him and bring a carrot!

My favorite picture and memory of baby **Caylan**, Matt and Laurie's firstborn. His favorite chore was "cawwats" for the horses! How PaPa loved to help him—the horses loved him too!

My two sons, Paul Jr. and Matthew, on Matt's wedding day, August 25, 1985. You have to be a father of two fine young sons like these to know the joy they bring. Now you can see where they got their good looks!

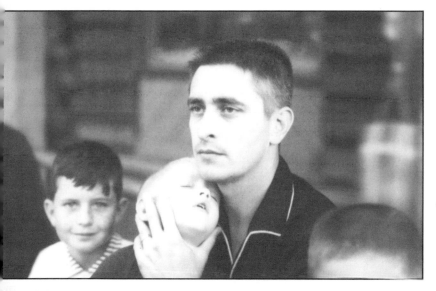

My advise to parents: cherish and enjoy those precious moments and treasures. They are your gifts from the Lord; but, oh—they are grown and gone too soon!

Our attorneys, Colby May (left) and Timothy Dyk (right) the day we presented our TV license challenge to the Federal Court in Washington, D.C.—February 29, 2000. On May 5, 2000, the three-judge panel voted 3 to 0 to give us back all TV licenses. PTL, PTL—forever!

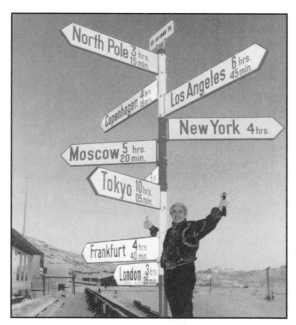

Hello World—Here we come again!

my hosts thought I was ill, or at least receiving some kind of tragic news.

Mr. Gammon said, "Paul—" an eternity passed between my name and the next word! "I have GOOD NEWS!"

The bells of heaven rang! I heard the *"Hallelujah Chorus"!* I shouted and then dropped the phone!

Jim continued, "A telegram is on the way from the FCC—your license for Channel 40 has been *GRANTED!"*

As quickly as I could excuse myself, I headed for my hotel room! There, I threw myself across the bed as I wept my thanks and praise to God. It was there that the Lord gave me one of the most precious words I have ever received. As I do so often, I flipped my Bible open and this verse leaped off the page:

> *He hath delivered my soul in peace from the battle that was against me: for there were many with me. (Psalm 55:18)*

I rushed home—August 2, 1974—to await the call from Western Union that the telegram had arrived. Another eternity passed, but at about 3 P.M. the call came! As I roared out the drive-way to personally pick up the telegram, Jan and Joshua (our big, white German shepherd) were actually doing a *DANCE* out on the patio—I am sure it was in the Spirit! I could hear her clear down the street laughing and crying—"Josh, we got it! Josh, we got it!"

We will never forget that night—*August 2, 1974*—as we read the telegram on *Praise the Lord!* Our joy overflowed as God's people from all over Southern California claimed THEIR TV STATION in Jesus' name!

One of our partners, Loraine Napier, expressed perfectly the great joy we all felt flooding our souls:

> *Dearest Paul and Jan: Whoever heard tell of one on a welfare grant owning a TV station? Well, I do! My Heavenly Father bought me one tonight! P.T.L.— Fantastic! Imagine me, a financial nobody, suddenly part owner of not only the CATTLE on the hill, but the HILL itself! There's a chunk of Mt. Wilson up there tonight which actually belongs to us! Can you believe it? Talk about the unsearchable riches of God!*

Now the station was ours and the hard work began in earnest. Weeks of preparation in anticipation of this great day had already laid a good programming foundation. Jan and cohost Sally Holiday did a ladies' program called *Happiness Is*. Pastor Ed Smith did a Bible study along with Dr. Robert Frost. Delbert Hosteller did a sign language program for the deaf; the Catholics did *It's a Brand New Day;* and yes, I continued the second oldest program even to this date—*Behind the Scenes*. Some of the programs had been planned, but not actually produced. But now we all rolled up our sleeves and began the joyful task of creating *CHRISTIAN TELEVISION* for *ALL* of Southern California.

One small change in the programming brought me more personal satisfaction than just about any other. For months, as we had been purchasing the airtime from Mr. Lerma, at the end of every *Praise the Lord* program the station ran a "disclaimer" that read: "The views expressed on the preceding program do not necessarily reflect the views of the staff and management of Channel 40 TV." The announcement had always grated on my nerves—especially on nights when we had seen a mighty move of the Spirit of God. When we finally took possession of *OUR TV STATION,* I got my revenge! I changed the *DISCLAIMER* to what I called a *"CLAIMER"* that now read: *"The views expressed on the preceding program do MOST DEFINITELY express the views of the staff and management of Channel 40!"* We all got a chuckle from that one!

The next several months and even on into 1975 were happy, productive, and busy months. Our board, which still consisted of Norm Juggert, Paul Toberty, and myself, worked beautifully together as Channel 40 began to bloom! Paul, who was a general contractor and an excellent businessman, helped us make plans for our very own studio building just across the line from Santa Ana in Tustin, California. We were finally able to lease a one-and-a-half-acre lot in a new industrial development that was being built by the giant Irvine Company.

Paul also strongly recommended that we add a new board member, brother Demos Shakarian, well known as the founder and president of the Full Gospel Businessmen's Fellowship International. Paul had been an international director and chapter president for several years, and he felt that Brother Demos's presence on the board would add credibility and strength to TBN.

I was not too enthusiastic at first—I had been hurt and stymied by differing goals and visions for TBN by several earlier board members—but Norm and I finally yielded to Paul's desire

and welcomed Brother Demos Shakarian as an official member
of the board of directors for TBN. Demos brought even more
valuable business experience to our work and for a time helped
TBN immensely as we entered our first phase of rapid growth.

❦

About this same time, the Lord began to deal with my heart concerning the breach of fellowship that I had personally suffered
with Pastor Ralph Wilkerson. My children, listen up—another
lesson to be learned. Without really realizing it—or at least
unwilling to admit it—I had carried a real root of bitterness
toward Pastor Ralph. In my mind he had tried to take TBN away
from Jan and me. I was convinced that if he ever did gain total
control of TBN that she and I would be history! I am sure now
that in Ralph's mind he felt he was doing the very best thing for
the good of TBN and the Kingdom of God.

One day the Lord spoke very clearly and said: *"You are to call
Pastor Ralph Wilkerson and ask him to forgive you."* The word not
only startled me but also displeased me! After all, didn't God
know that it was Ralph that had hurt *ME?* I was the totally innocent, wounded party—I should have an apology from Ralph! But
as the Lord continued to deal with my heart, He reminded me of
the scriptural command that if our brother offends us—we are to
go to him (Matthew 18:15)—I was to take the initiative.

Finally I called. I asked Pastor Ralph if he would meet me for
lunch. I am sure he wondered just what Paul Crouch wanted with
this request for a luncheon meeting, but he readily agreed.

Neither of us ate any lunch that day as I simply opened my heart to Ralph and confessed the bitterness I had held toward him through our trials and tribulations. It was one of the most difficult things that God had ever required me to do, but I finally said, "Ralph, will you forgive me?"

Tears welled up in Ralph's eyes as he graciously accepted my apology and then offered one of his own, as he asked me to forgive him for any perceived hurt or injury. Ralph and I have since stood together many times on the platforms of great Christian gatherings. He has appeared on *Praise the Lord* and other programs. The wounds and sorrows of the past are healed as both ministries have moved on in building the Kingdom.

My children, I am convinced that TBN would not have been successful had I not obeyed the Lord and asked for Ralph's forgiveness. Always remember the old adage: *"It is the little foxes that spoil the vine."*

🦅

Now things really began to explode at TBN. By mid-1975 our new studio building was fully under way. We would finally have a home studio of our own—so necessary if we were ever to have *TWENTY-FOUR-HOUR-A-DAY* Christian television.

I remember taking Papa Bethany, Jan's dad, out to the bare piece of ground before construction had begun. Weeds were waist high as we walked the four corners of the property. Finally he knelt down and with hands raised high, he declared, "This shall be the *WORLD HEADQUARTERS OF TRINITY BROADCASTING*

NETWORK!" After prayer and praise, he picked up a small clump of dirt, folded it neatly in his handkerchief, and vowed to pray every day for TBN!

What a saint, our Papa Bethany, and how we miss him and his prayers today. He went home to heaven in October of 1975, but he had lived to see the miracle of Channel 40 and the new studio walls going up.

Now, in addition to a new studio, other awesome opportunities began to present themselves. Mr. Gammon, our FCC attorney, called one day and advised me that UHF TV allocations were opening up in many major cities across America. As a result, we filed applications for Houston, Denver, and Seattle. In early 1976, an opportunity opened to purchase an existing station, Channel 21, in Phoenix, Arizona. Later an application was filed for Oklahoma City. The story of each of these great stations could fill a book of its own as we went through many of the same trials and tribulations we had gone through with Channel 40!

I will never know for sure just why, but this flurry of activity and growth began to disturb Demos Shakarian, and since he and Paul Toberty were so closely related in the Full Gospel Businessmen, Paul, too, began to question all of this rapid growth. Jan and I became increasingly perplexed, along with Norm Juggert, as to why everyone was not just as excited as we were about the possibility of new growth and *more stations!*

As I told you earlier, in retrospect, I believe that much of the Christian leadership actually feared that Christian TV could become a serious drain on the overall finances of the churches and parachurch organizations. I think the perception was, and may still be, that there is only a limited amount of dollars out there and that TBN might cut the pie thinner for them. Time has surely disproved this as numerous new ministries and new megachurches have arisen these past thirty years along with Christian television.

I do recall Demos saying on one occasion, "Paul, why do you have to pull so hard for finances on your telethons? You are pulling too hard for money!"

I had never perceived that we were "pulling too hard"—most of the telethons were times of great refreshing and more like old-time revival. It was true, however, that TBN's finances were going up at an awesome pace. We had finally hit pledges of a *MILLION DOLLARS* in the fall 1976 Praise-a-Thon!

Finally, at a board meeting I shall never forget, Demos looked at me sternly and said, "Paul, you will not build any more TV stations—ONE STATION is enough!"

Jan and I were devastated once again and there ensued, dear children, another valley of testing and despair. And yet, in the end—well, here I go, getting ahead of my story again!

CHAPTER SEVENTEEN

AND I SAW ANOTHER ANGEL

LOOKING BACK THESE THIRTY YEARS, IT IS AMAZING to see that in spite of changing board members, in spite of struggles for control, and in spite of conflicting ideas and goals for the ministry—TBN continued to *GROW* at an incredible pace. This was, and surely is, God's miracle that had been confirmed by a beautiful word of prophecy given at one of our rallies in the early days of TBN. Jerry Barnard, who was, at the time, pastor of Christian Faith Center in San Diego, had given this most encouraging word of prophecy, which was recorded on tape and later transcribed word for word:

> *The Lord Himself would say unto you—the investment of time and money, the investments of life and blood itself that you have made for My cause have been noted by the*

*Lord and have been taken note of even in the record books
of heaven. Fear not; neither seek the applause nor the
praise of men, for they will not always understand your
vision. But believe and know that what I have willed,
and what I have begun, no man can stop, and no man
can detour, and no man can take away. For I, the Lord,
will cause My work to prosper and grow, and there will
be no storm, there will be no great power that will come
against My will, that will overpower it. For I will accomplish the work that I have set forth to do. For I am the
Lord and it is My work, saith the Lord God Almighty.*

The date was June 15, 1975.

❦

A few months later, in October of 1975, I remember so clearly
reflecting on the future of TBN in the den of our home. I knew
in my spirit we would one day have a network of TV stations
across the continent. We were already filing applications with the
FCC to accomplish this in spite of board objections and directives. But I did *not* expect, in my wildest dreams, the awesome
revelation that came to me that Saturday afternoon!

As I was praying and seeking the Lord for the future of TBN,
that familiar voice spoke again! This time it came in the form of
a vision so vivid and startling, I had to catch my breath. I saw on
the ceiling of our den a giant map of the United States. Hovering
high above it was a bright light, and issuing from it were beautiful streams of light moving toward the outline of the map. The

streams of light then began to strike the major population centers: Los Angeles, Miami, New York, Seattle, and so on until the whole country was surrounded. As the streams of light landed, secondary lights were illuminated, and then, in extremely rapid succession, small, threadlike streams of light began to spread out. As they spread, little dots of light began to glow until the whole map was literally bathed in a network of lights!

I sat there transfixed by what I was seeing as I cried out to God to show me what all this meant. As I waited upon the Lord, He spoke one ringing, resounding word to my spirit—*"SATELLITE!"*

"But, how, Lord? When, Lord?" I began to cry.

"Soon," came the voice of the Lord. *"VERY SOON."*

As the vision faded from my consciousness, only then did the enormity of it all begin to settle in upon me, filling my very spirit, soul, and body with an excitement and anticipation I had never known before!

A few nights later God confirmed my vision through Pastor John Hinkle, pastor of Christ Church in Los Angeles. John was our guest on *Praise the Lord* as God began to move in mighty healing power. The prayer lines were literally jammed as calls came pouring in from all over Southern California. *"Praise God, I'm healed of arthritis! I can move without pain!"* *"My left ear just popped open—I have been deaf for fourteen years!"* *"My tumor has just disappeared—right before my eyes!"*

Before the program ended, more than *250 testimonies* had been received, praising God for miraculous and instantaneous healings! But God was not through revealing His word of knowledge that night. As Pastor Hinkle drove home in the wee hours of the morning, the Spirit of the Lord came so powerfully upon him, he told us later, that he had to pull his car to a stop off the freeway. God said, *"What you have seen tonight of My healing power, you can multiply ONE HUNDREDFOLD! I will indeed* raise *up a mighty network of stations across America!"*

Here again was God's mighty confirmation of His glorious plan—a gigantic Christian television network that would, as the old hymn says, "give the winds a mighty voice!" Praise God, thirty years later, this word of the Lord has come to pass. As of 2003, we have more than 4,000 TV and radio stations ON THE AIR worldwide. Praise God! One hundredfold indeed! Pastor John is in heaven today, but he lived to see most of that awesome word of knowledge come to pass.

Not long after my vision and several confirmations by other men and women of God, I was contacted by RCA Americom, the *satellite division* of the RCA corporation. They were preparing to launch their first television communications satellite, so they called on me to see if TBN would be interested in acquiring a channel on SATCOM I to feed our TV network to the growing number of cable stations, plus any other broadcast stations that we might acquire in the future!

I remember my heart skipped another beat when the contract was presented—$34,000 a month for a full twenty-four-hour-a-day channel! *Dear Lord, our whole budget was less than that a month,* but by faith I signed it—committing to one whole channel on

"ANGEL I," as we called it, which was to be launched in the next few months.

Now we would have to file for the most exciting FCC license of all—a SATELLITE TV station that would cover the whole North American continent! The industry was so new that the FCC did not even have any satellite application forms prepared as yet. But we applied anyway! Our FCC attorney helped us, and with our engineer's input, we filed for the *FIRST* Southern California satellite station.

I'm sure many will remember the great excitement as we raised the funds in the fall of 1977 for this most awesome step of faith yet for TBN. Next, the huge ten-meter dish was ordered, plus all of the exotic electronics to go with it. Then came the wait, as usual, for the FCC to process our application. Days dragged into weeks, and weeks into months. Each time we would call our FCC attorney, the word was the same—"next month," then "next week," then "next Monday" and so on. For nearly six months this was the pattern.

Finally, we were desperate. Every time I drove in and out of the parking lot, the huge pile of packing crates containing the satellite equipment would confront me. It seemed as though this mountain of equipment was mocking me. Thousands of dollars' worth of equipment sitting there, ready to go . . . but no FCC authority to build.

To make matters even worse, word came from our attorney that the FCC might be reviewing this whole concept of satellite authorizations; it might be referred "upstairs" to the full Commission for action. That could take many more months— my heart sank within me.

Dear Lord, another "Red Sea"—another impossible situation, I thought. The final word from our attorney on Thursday morning, February 16, 1978, was "Paul, I have no news . . ."

The sick feeling in the pit of my stomach deepened. "Maybe next week—Tuesday or Wednesday." He tried to sound reassuring. At about 6 P.M., I went into my office, locked the door, and lay prostrate before the Lord. As I agonized in prayer, God showed me clearly what to do. Remember God's promise:

> *And ye shall seek me, and find me, when ye shall search
> for me with all your heart. (Jeremiah 29:13)*

❦

As I have said so often, God delights to allow these impossible situations to prove HIS mighty power to deliver!

The *Praise the Lord* program was live that night—Jan and I were hosting. Back then, it began at 9 P.M., so for nearly three hours I interceded for His direction. As I prayed, the Lord showed me that we should turn the whole *Praise the Lord* program into one gigantic prayer meeting. You see, He wanted all of the TBN partners to be a part of His next great miracle!

At nine o'clock the familiar *Praise the Lord* theme echoed out across the airwaves. Jan and I poured out our hearts and burdens to the most wonderful partners in the world. The *PTL* chairs and table were moved back out of the way as we knelt before the Lord and began to pray.

Thousands joined in as we sought the Lord with all our hearts. Jim and Carol Hampton were our guests that night, along with

Dr. Russell Spittler from Fuller Theological Seminary. What a glorious prayer meeting we had! Many other unannounced guests, including Jerry and Sandy Barnard, simply stopped by, led to come that night by the Holy Spirit.

At about midnight, the burden lifted—we knew God had heard the cry of His children. We had, as the old-timers say, *"PRAYED THROUGH"!* But we never dreamed how quickly the answer would come. Oh, we of "little faith"!

The very next day, Friday morning, an urgent call reached me. The operator advised—"WASHINGTON, D.C., calling."

It can't be this soon, I thought.

"Paul, I can't believe it, but . . ." The excitement in Jim Gammon's voice was unmistakable. "We have your construction permit from the FCC for your new satellite station!"

"But how?" I exclaimed.

Jim replied, "I simply don't know, Paul. I have never experienced anything like this in all my legal career—it has to be God's miracle!" And for our FCC attorney, that was quite a confession!

Joy flowed like a mighty river as we flashed the good news to our TBN partners the very next night. Another MIGHTY STATION was born! The answer had come in only *TWELVE* hours!

In days, the giant ten-meter earth satellite dish was hoisted onto its foundation. Its gleaming white frame tilted at an unusually high angle, ready to probe the heavens in search of its target. The target: a wing-shaped package of highly sophisticated electronic wonders—22,000 miles above the equator in stationary orbit—yes, "ANGEL I" was flying high, and now—wonder of wonders—we could talk to it.

That night the Lord gave us a prophetic promise from His Word:

> *Ask of Me, and I will give You the nations for Your inher-*
> *itance, And the ends of the earth for Your possession.*
> *(Psalm 2:8 NKJV)*

Yes, God gave us HIS mighty *satellite angel* to reach our world with the Gospel of Christ. God knew that OUR generation would be the first generation to fulfill this glorious prophecy.

As the Lord would have it, our first transmission would be an "earnest" of that inheritance. On April 10, 1978, at the National Association of Broadcasters Convention in Las Vegas, Nevada, we sent our first full *Praise the Lord* program to all of the exhibitors. Hundreds of secular broadcasters from all over the nation received the Gospel—we were finally HEAVEN BOUND!

NO MORE STATIONS

MY CHILDREN, AS I TOLD YOU AT THE BEGINNING of this account, the worst pain always seems to come from those you love the most. Surely this next chapter confirms that sad reality.

Demos Shakarian was one of the giants of the faith! Through the years he shared the miracle birth of the Full Gospel Businessmen's Fellowship International many times on TBN and, of course, in countless banquets, conventions, and books. Demos and his wife, Rose, were living legends as their great work spread around the world. The testimony of Demos's calling from the Lord was just as miraculous as the call Jan and I had received, and we always held him and the work of the Full Gospel Businessmen in highest esteem.

But as I explained earlier, the explosive growth of TBN became a matter of great concern to Demos, as well as his close associate,

Paul Toberty. I was determined to seize every opportunity to expand the ministry of TBN, so as applications were filed for more TV stations, we naturally had to expend TBN funds for attorney fees, engineering services, filing fees, plus the costs of forming new corporations. In those days, the FCC looked more favorably on your application if you applied through a corporation that was domiciled in the same state as the TV station. Thus we formed Trinity of Arizona, Trinity of Florida, Trinity of New York, and so on.

Since Demos and Paul were 50 percent of the board, they had *de facto* veto power over myself and Norm Juggert. By the way, this was a very unhealthy combination—that is why most all institutions, from the Supreme Court all the way down to the smallest city council, have an odd number of members; otherwise similar deadlocks can occur.

Finally, at our next board meeting, I was ordered not to expend any more funds on these newly emerging corporations. I was told that it was improper to transfer funds from one corporation to another without board approval. To make matters even worse, members of the Full Gospel Businessmen in Oklahoma City, Houston, and Seattle, who had been very supportive at first, now refused to assist us in our efforts to acquire stations in those cities.

Jan and I were frustrated again as we could see no way to move on with what we knew was the vision for TBN. Finally, in prayer, the idea of spinning the *Praise the Lord* program off into a separate department came to me. After all, this program was unquestionably the main driving force of the ministry, and the one I had been solely responsible for. Also, most of the funds coming into TBN were a result of the *Praise the Lord* program, so a specially designated fund was created for *Praise the Lord,* which gave us the ability to pursue the dream of a television network that I knew would one day span the continent.

When this was discussed in a board meeting, Demos and Paul were not, at all, in agreement. They knew I was deliberately circumventing the authority of the board, and they demanded, and then unilaterally ordered, an audit of the books by an outside certified public accounting firm. I felt this was a waste of much-needed funds, knowing that we had done nothing wrong and that all funds could be properly accounted for. Norm Juggert tried vainly to be the peacemaker and the mediator, but the sad truth was we were locked in disagreement, once again, for control of the future of TBN.

❦

How sad that even within the Body of Christ, when confidence and trust is lost in each other, all kinds of tragic thoughts, feelings, and actions are the result. I truly believed that Demos and Paul were hoping that the audit would reveal some impropriety or illegal action so that they would have justification for removing me from the board.

Demos and Paul selected the accounting firm, and for several days they pored over the books and records of TBN. They examined the daily deposits of donor mail, checked bank accounts, asked me many questions, and finally submitted their report.

What the report showed clearly was that funds had simply flowed through the *Praise the Lord* account and that all TBN bills had been paid, as usual, in a timely manner. It showed that we had indeed continued to expend funds for the growth and development of TBN, and that every penny had been spent in accordance with the IRS-exempt purpose of the corporation. In fact, much of the funds had been expended for the expansion of TBN in accordance with the designation of the donors. This was only natural since we were asking our partners to give for specific new areas of outreach such as Phoenix, Oklahoma City, and Seattle.

When the two TBN accounts were finally reconciled, there was a slight difference of about eleven dollars, which the auditors said was a simple bookkeeping error on our part.

When the report was read at our next board meeting, I honestly saw disappointment registered on Demos and Paul's faces; but of course, only God could truly have known what was in their hearts. At this board meeting, however, we had a new attendee: *JANICE BETHANY CROUCH!* While she was not an actual voting member of the board, she nevertheless demanded to be heard at this meeting. We learned later that most of the employees of TBN were *de facto* attendees at this part of the board meeting, since her voice was clearly heard up and down the hall! The obstructionist tactics of Demos and Paul were now apparent to all, and Jan had had it, too!

There is a little saying still around TBN that goes like this: "Which would you rather have: Jan's wrath or God's wrath?" Most staffers prefer God's wrath, since it holds the promise of much more mercy!

"Where were YOU, Demos Shakarian, when God spoke to Paul Crouch and me simultaneously and called us to this ministry?" she

shouted. *"Where were YOU when we were scraping tile and tar off the floor of our first studio?"*

Now her voice was rising and the tears began to flow! *"Where were YOU, Paul Toberty, when God moved a mountain for us and brought in $35,000 the day of our deadline for Channel 40? Where were you BOTH when God gave Paul Crouch the VISION of satellite and TV stations linked together covering the land with Christian television?"* She sobbed.

My God, as tough an old German as I am, I was ready to crawl under a chair somewhere! I think Norm Juggert was not far behind! I have to confess that this was the most anointed rebuke I had ever witnessed. Jan's Irish eyes were not smiling—they were flashing water and fire! Her grandmother, Annie Laurie Greene, would have been proud of her!

At the conclusion of that meeting, the fight was over—the steam had dissipated—the *coup*, if it had been one, had failed. For several minutes you could have heard a pin drop all over the building. Pale-faced employees, who had heard every word of my sweetheart's eruption, worked feverishly at their desks. We probably got more work done that afternoon than the rest of the whole week!

Finally, Demos Shakarian spoke. "Jan," he said, "you are right. Perhaps we should all think and pray about the future of TBN."

With that, we adjourned, but it was a NEW DAY for TBN. We had passed an important milestone. Even the atmosphere—the air itself—was different. TBN would go forward.

But the story is far from over. Remember, I told you this episode has an amazing ending!

CHAPTER NINETEEN

"THE BARREN HATH BORN SEVEN"

MIRACULOUSLY, IN SPITE OF EVERY DIFFICULTY, IN spite of all the dissension and strife, TBN continued to grow! God even gave us a powerful word of prophecy as Jan and Joyce Toberty were interceding in prayer for TBN in the den of our home. By the Holy Spirit, they were directed to the book of Samuel and the prayer of Hannah:

> *Those who were hungry cease to hunger.*
> *Even the barren gives birth to seven. (1 Samuel 2:5 NASB)*

I was ecstatic at this word since, at this time, the maximum number of full-power TV stations permitted by the FCC to one owner was *SEVEN!* I knew in my spirit that we would have these stations, but this was glorious confirmation. And now, with Demos and Paul in agreement after our traumatic board meeting, we were finally on our way!

Shortly after this promise was given, we were contacted by a group of businessmen from Phoenix, Arizona. Channel 21 had been purchased by Pastor Lindell Edmonds of Bible Fellowship Church, but it was having serious financial problems. Over two million dollars had been raised through the sale of bonds and the church was in default. After many meetings and negotiating sessions, TBN agreed to assume all debts of the station in exchange for the license and assets. This was an awesome responsibility for TBN. It was December of 1975 and we had only been on the air with Channel 40, our first TV station, for a little over a year!

I will never forget that historic meeting with about three hundred mostly elderly people who had invested their savings in a Christian TV station that was now unable to pay them back. We had been sending *Praise the Lord* and a few other programs over to Phoenix and purchasing some airtime, so they were basically familiar with TBN, but we were so new—*could we ever pay them back?*

Jan and I poured out our hearts and vision for a great Christian television network to those precious saints on a Saturday afternoon in Phoenix. We promised that we would work till our fingers bled and pray till our knees were calloused to pay them every penny plus interest!

Finally, a vote was to be taken, but before ballots could even be passed out, an elderly gentleman stood up and said, "I've heard enough. I believe Paul and Jan will come through—I vote to accept their plan and sell Channel 21 to TBN!" With that, the entire group burst into applause and it was settled. TBN would be endorsed by the bondholders to take control of KPAZ-TV Channel 21 Phoenix, Arizona!

❧

But there were still may hurdles to be crossed. Word spread that TBN had made application to the FCC for the purchase of Channel 21. My children, believe it or not, it was some Christian brothers that nearly destroyed our whole plan for station number two! This time it was from two different sources.

Jim Bakker was developing a successful TV ministry back in North Carolina, as we have already discussed. Jim was also pondering the prospect of purchasing whole TV stations for the expansion of his PTL Club and Heritage USA ministry. So he sent his representative to Phoenix and entered into negotiations with Pastor Lindell Edmonds for the purchase of Channel 21. At about the same time, David Yonggi Cho, from Seoul, South Korea, entered the picture. He, too, through American partners, contacted Pastor Edmonds and entered into negotiations as well.

Yes, even the greatest men of God have feet of clay! All of us who are called of God can miss the perfect will of God at times. I do not cry down from any ivory tower since I, too, have missed the will of God at times, but I tell you of this sad chapter to warn you of the importance of seeking and knowing the PERFECT will of God at each and every point in your lives.

What followed is another dark chapter in this first expansion of the miracle of TBN. Pastor Edmonds sent a letter canceling our original agreement to purchase Channel 21, which dashed our hopes and dreams for station number two and the next phase of a great network of stations spanning the continent. For several months it looked as though Channel 21 was finished. Finally the RCA corporation, who owned the main transmission equipment, moved in and repossessed the transmitter. Now the station was off the air!

I will never forget how discouraged and depressed I had been to receive this news. It seemed now that all was lost and that Channel 21 would never be ours.

In the midst of this sickening news, our pastor, Jack Hayford, had come to be our special guest on *Praise the Lord*. Jack was, and still is, pastor of the historic Church on the Way in Van Nuys, California.

A few years earlier at a TBN staff meeting at which Pastor Jack was ministering, the Lord had spoken an important word to me. Kneeling in prayer beside me, I had turned to Pastor Jack and had asked him to be my pastor, as well as a spiritual covering for TBN. He graciously consented and with Anna, his wife, has been a source of wise and godly counsel to Jan and me through the years.

Before the program that night, Jan and I had poured out our hearts to our pastor. We had explained how unfairly we were being treated. We went into great detail, telling how we had already invested over $300,000 in the Phoenix station. That we had supplied much of the programming—had signed a legal contract—had filed our FCC application, only to have the contract broken by the owners.

Jack finally interrupted me in the middle of my tirade and gave me a word that shocked me! It was a word that I did not want to hear and at first could not receive. "Paul," he said gently, "give it up."

At first it did not even register—*give WHAT up?*

My pastor went on to explain. "You and Jan are trying to do this in your own strength. You have got to give Phoenix up to the Lord. Tell God that Phoenix is over—a closed chapter in your life."

Well, for an old *"Attila the Hun"* fighting German, this was not what I wanted to hear! I was ready to sue for specific performance—we had a signed contract—it was easily enforceable in a court of law! After several moments of rather stunned silence, I at least agreed for Jack to lead us in a time of prayer. I will confess that at this point I did not feel like praying. I was angry!

But gradually, the presence of the Holy Spirit began to soften my heart. Jan began to weep softly and finally Pastor Jack said, "Paul, will you follow me in a prayer of release?"

Reluctantly I agreed—it was one of the hardest prayers I have ever prayed. *"Dear Lord"*—I repeated phrase by phrase—*"I forgive all those who have hurt me."* I choked a little on that one.

"Father, we give Phoenix up to you . . . "

Swallowing hard, Jan and I both repeated: *"We give Phoenix up . . . "* A strange new peace settled upon us—the heavy burden lifted—Phoenix was now in God's hands. In my mind Phoenix was gone—forever!

But now, once again, it was God's move! Ah, if ever we could truly learn that the battle is the Lord's!

Since the equipment had been repossessed and the station was off the air, the situation was getting desperate. Lawsuits were being filed by bondholders against the owners. The license was even in jeopardy since the FCC will not allow a station to remain off the air indefinitely. TBN partners were so incensed at the developments, they brought pressure on the owners, even picketing the station, demanding that the purchase contract with TBN be renewed!

Finally Pastor Edmonds was back at the table, willing to work out a new contract for TBN to assume ownership of Channel 21! After several more difficult negotiating sessions, we hammered out a new and much better contract for TBN.

By now, the folks at the Phoenix airport were getting to know me—not from being on TV either! Since the financial needs of many of the elderly bondholders was getting desperate, my FCC attorney and I paid a personal visit on all the Arizona senators and congressmen. We asked them to do an unprecedented favor for TBN—to write a joint letter to the FCC urging speedy consideration of TBN's new contract and application for the license of KPAZ-TV in Phoenix.

To our great delight, Senators Barry Goldwater and Dennis DeConcini, along with all of the Arizona congressmen, agreed and signed the very special request to the chairman of the FCC, Mr. Richard Wiley.

The wait was agonizing, as always, but now because of this special assistance from Congress, we had hope that a decision would come soon. *And soon it was!* In weeks, rather than months, the telegram was flashed: *COMMISSION GRANTED!* The date—July 21, 1977. Arizona and California rejoiced—Channel 21 would be ours—and what a date: *7/21/77!*

Now came the final phase—close of escrow. This is where the property deeds were transferred, attorney fees paid, the new bond payment schedule set up, plus a thousand and one miscellaneous transactions were completed. It was here that Satan made his last stand to stop the transfer—to yet deny TBN station number two.

Because so much time had passed since our original agreement, a number of the bondholders had reached the end of their patience. They now demanded payment in full, and some of them were board members of the station whose signatures would be required for the closing documents. Others had filed earlier lawsuits and had been awarded judgments by the court. The cries and demands of a few turned into a veritable three-ring circus as they realized that the FCC had approved the license transfer and now this was a real sale!

I must say here that the vast majority of bondholders were precious and generous beyond words! They had agreed to a semiannual payback with interest over a twelve-year period! Some even voluntarily donated some or all of their bonds back to TBN! God bless them! Many have since gone home to Glory—what a reward they have entered into! *More than twenty million souls through TBN (that we know of) are credited to their account!*

We finally reached agreement with all but one of the bondholders. I will never forget this final, traumatic meeting in the office of his attorney. He demanded $25,000 in cash or the whole new deal was off! I was angry and incensed that "Christians" would take advantage of this sensitive and critical final stage of our closing, but that was it—their final offer!

I asked for a few minutes to think and pray for direction. This seemed to be literally the straw that would break the camel's back! *"Dear Lord,"* I cried. *"What now?"* The truth was, we did not have the $25,000—besides, even the debt we were assuming looked large and frightening. My faith truly began to waiver.

I called my prayer partner back home in California. I said, "Honey, I don't believe we can handle this. These last bondholders won't budge. They are demanding all cash and we just do not have it." I also explained that under the terms of our agreement, these bondholders could actually prevent the closing of escrow and, in effect, the whole deal for Channel 21!

Over the phone we began to pray and, as usual, Jan began to cry. As we called out to God for help and direction, she suddenly cried out. At first I wasn't sure if it was a cry of praise or despair! "Honey," she cried, "I just opened my Bible—listen to this!" The Scripture was from the prophet Haggai 2:1:

In the seventh month, in the one and twentieth day of the month . . .

Dear Lord, regardless of what followed, I immediately recognized that DATE! The FCC had granted the transfer of the license in the *"SEVENTH MONTH"* and on the *"ONE AND TWENTIETH DAY"*—yes, July 21, 1977! But there was more—much more!

Who is left among you that saw this house in her first glory? And how do ye see it now? Is it not in your eyes in comparison of it as nothing? (Haggai 2:3)

How true! Channel 21 was off the air. It was indeed "AS NOTHING"! But here is where it exploded in our spirits:

> *Yet now be strong . . . saith the LORD . . . Be strong, all*
> *ye people of the land, saith the LORD, and work: for I am*
> *with you, saith the LORD of hosts. (Haggai 2:4)*

As the text continued, it was the same as if God Himself was speaking directly to us:

> *I will fill this house with glory, saith the Lord of hosts . . .*

And here was the clincher—my answer to the financial demands:

> *The silver is mine, and the gold is mine . . . The glory of*
> *this latter house shall be greater than the former . . . and*
> *in this place will I give peace, saith the LORD of hosts.*
> *(Haggai 2:7, 8–9)*

By now, Jan and I were both weeping and shouting our praises to God! K"PAZ"—*paz* means "peace" in Spanish—God's final word was "In this place will I give peace!" That was it—I had my answer—I went back into the attorney's office and said, "It's a deal. Where do I sign?"

❦

I knew God would provide the money—CHANNEL 21 was ours again only by His miracle. I do not even remember where the money came from, but it was there when we needed it and we *CLOSED THE ESCROW,* changed all the locks on the doors, and went crazy with joy putting Channel 21 BACK ON THE AIR. Our engineers worked literally around the clock to reassemble all the equipment that had been repossessed, and in a little more than a month KPAZ-TV Channel 21 in Phoenix, Arizona, flashed ON THE AIR with "LET'S JUST PRAISE THE LORD!"

And while in many other places we have had more troubles and trials—true to His word, in Phoenix, God has given us *HIS "PAZ"!*

After all the excitement of Channel 21, the very next year perhaps the most far-reaching and exciting TV station was born. Yes, it was in 1978 that the great satellite station came on the air, which I told you about earlier. Soon after, in 1980, we bought Lester Sumrall's full-power station in Miami! What a night that was as we threw the first coast-to-coast switch and linked East and West together—LIVE—for the first time in Christian television history!

One interesting sidelight to our purchase of Channel 45 in Miami was where the down payment came from. As our partners knew, we had agreed to pay Lester Sumrall $10 MILLION dollars for his station. The good news was that he financed half of the purchase price at no interest. But we still had to have $5 million dollars at the close of escrow, and we had only half of what we needed, or about $2.5 million dollars. Just as we needed the balance, I was approached by HBO.

If you have cable TV you know what *Home Box Office* is. They were getting started about the same time our satellite station came on the air. They had a very special need to be on the satellite we were accessing, but it was full—there was no more room. Since we were feeding mostly our own stations and a few affiliates, it really did not matter that much which satellite we were on. I consulted with Jim Gammon, our FCC attorney, as to how much he thought we should charge them for the switch in satellites. He thought maybe up to $1.5 million dollars. After all, satellite was brand new, no one really knew its value.

I said, "Jim, I need $2.5 million dollars for Miami!"

Jim swallowed hard, but agreed to present the demand. To our great joy and surprise, they accepted without even haggling, giving us the other half of the $5 million dollars needed for our down payment on Miami! *Miami, you were expensive, but you were worth it! And, by the way, Satan hated and feared you the most, as we shall soon see!*

One more miracle I have to share while dealing with Miami concerns the huge antenna that sits atop the thousand-foot supporting tower.

A short time after we closed the escrow with Lester Sumrall, the antenna and feed line caught fire and burned out! This was a terrible shock, since the repair bill came to about $350,000! So we had no choice—equipment was ordered and installation begun. Apart from the day God moved a mountain for us, this amazing story I'm about to tell you is surely one of the greatest physical and most visible miracles of all!

✑

The engineers decided the antenna should be lowered into place by a large, military-style helicopter. Remember, we were dealing with a piece of equipment forty feet long and weighing over two tons! Since this was an extremely hazardous exercise, the trailer park residents living at the base of the thousand-foot TV tower had to be evacuated.

The helicopter pilot and engineer were a father-and-son team— Dad flew the chopper and the son was positioned atop the TV tower, waiting to bolt the huge antenna in place as soon as it was lowered. The cable connecting the antenna to the chopper was designed with a disconnect device that was activated with an explosive charge so that the chopper could break the cable and fly away once the antenna was secured in place. Father and son were communicating through a pair of two-way radios and all seemed to be going well as the giant helicopter hovered with its precious, but hazardous, burden. We would learn later that the two-way radio system had failed and that father and son had reverted to hand signals for communication.

My sister Naomi and her husband, Bernard Ridings, were managing the station at the time. He later gave us the picture from the ground as the four-story-tall antenna was lowered a few inches at a time. The pilot's son was waiting, poised to anchor the antenna base to its platform with bolts the size of dinner plates! Frantically, the son was trying to signal his father that he was having trouble getting the bolts to thread properly, but the father interpreted the signal to mean "All is well"! BANG! The explosive charge was triggered and the helicopter flew away with the forty-foot-tall, two-ton antenna standing on its platform, rocking precariously!

Panic-stricken, the son worked feverishly for several minutes, rotating the large bolts that would finally secure the antenna to its base.

Bernard, who was watching and praying at the bottom of the thousand-foot tower, told us that the Spirit of the Lord came upon him at this moment and that he began to pray mightily in the Spirit in an unknown tongue! From his vantage point all seemed to be going fine, but in his spirit he knew something was wrong!

The story that finally tumbled from an ashened-faced young engineer was a miracle of awesome proportions. With helicopter prop wash blowing full force on the unsecured antenna—*wonder of wonders*—it stood in a perfect upright position for several minutes until the final bolt was secured!

Father and son later likened this miracle to standing a long lead pencil on a table with a large fan blowing on it! They actually tried this experiment and could never get the pencil to stand! I am certain that if we could have looked into the invisible spirit world, we would have seen the hand of God holding that antenna in place.

We asked the young engineer if he knew how to pray and he exclaimed, "I do now! I learned how a thousand feet in the air when I heard that umbilical cord blow apart!"

For more than twenty years now, that miracle antenna has been beaming twenty-four-hour Christian television up and down the Gold Coast of south Florida. And every time I look up at that giant tower, a special praise to God leaps within my spirit! Yes, God will even override His own laws of physics to protect and keep those who are walking in His perfect will!

Oklahoma City came on the air in 1981 after a competing applicant finally withdrew. Next, Richmond/Cincinnati came on the air the same year, followed by New York in 1982, and finally

Seattle/Tacoma in 1984. I shall never forget that date for three very special reasons. First of all, as I explained earlier, in 1984 the maximum number of full-power stations any one organization could own was seven, and Seattle/Tacoma, Channel 20, was TBN's station number seven.

Secondly, it was March 30, 1984, my fiftieth birthday, when the news flashed—"KTBW-TV IS ON THE AIR!" We were hosting a great TBN rally from Hugh Rosenburg's Tri-County Assembly in Cincinnati. *What a night—what a birthday gift!* Our joy could hardly be contained! Seven great full-power stations and now affiliated stations were joining us, cable stations were hooking up, and even our low- and medium-power stations were coming on-line. And all linked together LIVE with our great new satellite station! To cap it all off, one brave partner stood up and began singing "Happy Birthday"—the whole congregation joined in—a highlight I will never forget!

But some very sad news reached us that night—my third reason for remembering it with very mixed emotions.

❦

In the middle of the live *Praise the Lord* program the call came— *"Brother Demos Shakarian has been rushed to the hospital in Los Angeles—a stroke—please pray!"* We immediately called the four thousand partners there, plus our TBN family from coast to coast, to intercession and prayer. The nation was shocked. Demos was one of our great leaders—a "father in Israel"—beloved by millions. Oh, how we prayed!

For several days we reported on his progress and, to our great joy, God heard and answered our prayers. This dairy farmer that God had used to raise up thousands of Full Gospel Businessmen's chapters around the world would live—he would continue to lead this great fellowship of businessmen to even greater heights. The Christian world rejoiced.

But the best part of this story, my children, I tell you now with even more joy than the joy of our seventh station signing on the air. Demos had gone through not only some physical deep waters, but also some political ones as well. His stroke had left him in a somewhat weakened condition, but his mind and spirit were perfectly intact—in fact, I have always believed, even stronger.

Now, it is one thing to have honest differences of opinion as to the direction and leadership of a ministry or organization, as was the case with Demos and TBN. But it is reprehensible to see ambitious, power-seeking *"Christians"* seek to unseat a God-ordained leader, such as Demos Shakarian, when he is down physically. But that is exactly what happened. A faction of the Full Gospel Businessmen felt that Demos should be "promoted" to "president emeritus" and, in effect, put out to pasture *(how's that for a good dairy term?).*

Jan and I finally learned of this problem and invited Demos to come and share his burden with the larger Body of Christ, so they could support and pray for him and the Full Gospel Businessmen. During this struggle for power *(dear Lord, when will this Body finally grow up?),* Demos appeared several times, and each time he grew stronger both in the Lord as well as in his rightful position as founder and president of Full Gospel Businessmen.

But on this first visit, something very special happened that Jan and I will treasure the rest of our lives. And Matt, my son, as the Lord would have it, you were there to be a witness.

At TBN, there is a long hall leading down to the *Praise the Lord* program set in what we call Studio C. Demos and his aide, who assisted him, had just stepped out of the washroom. Matt, you will recall that you just happened to descend the stairs and ended up a few steps behind Demos. At this point he was totally unaware of your presence.

Looking down from the hall, Demos spied Jan and me as we turned the corner, heading for the *Praise the Lord* set and the program that evening. We were excited that brother Demos was to be our special guest that night. The hall is not too brightly lit, but finally we could see Demos, who was waving and trying to get our attention. In hardly more than a hoarse whisper, he began to call out, "Paul and Jan, Paul and Jan!"

We quickened our pace and finally met at the door of Studio C. For a moment, I feared Demos was ill again as he reached out to grasp our hands. Tears welled up in this great man's eyes as he sobbed, "I'm sorry, I'm so sorry!"

We fell into each other's arms and wept our repentance and reconciliation. No explanation was needed—words would have gotten in the way—this was HEALING time—this was God's ordained rendezvous for three wounded souls that God wanted to mend. And mend us He did. Yes, Jan and I not only found the joy of reconciliation, but a new father in Christ! And Matt, I am so happy you got to be there and learn! Demos continued to serve as the rightful leader of the Fellowship for many more years until his home going in 1993.

The final joy to this chapter came with a most welcome letter from Paul Toberty shortly after this precious, God-ordained rendezvous. Demos Shakarian and Paul Toberty had both resigned from the board of TBN shortly after the traumatic board meeting I described in an earlier chapter. As might be expected, fellowship was broken, and what little relationship remained was strained at best. Gradually, hearts and spirits began to mend as we continued to work with and broadcast some of the great Full Gospel Businessmen's conventions. But the complete healing came in the form of that letter from Paul. It read in part as follows:

> It has been some time since we left TBN, but I felt that a letter of apology for any mistakes on my part, during our time there, was in order. Yet, I feel the Lord did place us there with you in the beginning, and had the assurance at the time that the ministry would have a great impact in the future. Certainly, this has come to pass.
>
> I trust this is accepted in the spirit in which it is written, as much as I want the best for you and your ministry, I, too want the same.

I was overjoyed to receive this wonderful word which, in my mind, completed any final healing which may have been needed. I immediately dictated a return letter which read in part:

> Dear Paul and Joyce: Thank you from both Jan and me for your refreshing and healing letter. You both have been much on my mind while I was writing an anniversary

book on the many trials and tribulations, but also the many joys and victories of TBN.

While Jan and I have long since forgiven and to a great deal forgotten our differences of the past, we still welcome your kind letter with all of our hearts.

We ask that you grant us the same forgiveness for anything that we may have done to cause hurt or sorrow in any of our relationship of the past.

So there you have it, my children, an important lesson on broken relationships—some of the causes, but also the marvelous cure for those who will hear and obey the command of Christ to FORGIVE.

I wish I could say that all of our problems and heartaches were over, but in a very real sense they were just beginning! Hold on, this next mountain is a big one!

CHAPTER TWENTY

SADDLEBACK

MY CHILDREN, WE COME NOW TO, WITHOUT A doubt, one of the most ominous threats ever raised against TBN, and for that matter against all Christian television. At least, in the first twenty years of TBN's history, nothing compared with *SADDLEBACK!*

By now, I have worn thin the phrase, "There came yet another valley of testing and despair!" Well, forget it—I won't—no, I can't use that phrase any more because this valley, at the time, had no equal! Up until then, at least, I was at differences with my Christian brothers. As traumatic as all of those encounters were—at least they were my brothers! I never feared for my actual physical life, but Saddleback was DIFFERENT!

But first, a little history so you will understand just how we reached this next crisis. Follow carefully, it gets a little complicated.

When we first bought Channel 40, it was licensed to a little suburb of Los Angeles called Fontana, California. Mr. Lerma, the owner, had received special permission from the FCC to operate his main studio in North Hollywood, which is in the city of Los Angeles. In those days, you were required to locate your main studio in your city of license, unless special permission was granted by the FCC to operate elsewhere. Remember, this all had nothing to do with your transmitter location which was, and still is, Mt. Wilson, next to all the other Southern California TV transmitters.

You will remember that TBN had been raised up in the city of Santa Ana, which is about fifty miles south of Los Angeles. Fontana is about fifty miles east of Los Angeles, so we wanted neither Fontana nor North Hollywood for our main studio location. We wanted to stay in Santa Ana or at least in Orange County, which is the large county just south of Los Angeles County.

Since Mr. Lerma had received permission to move his main studio into Los Angeles, we felt the FCC would have no objection to our asking for permission to operate our main studio right where we were in Santa Ana. But when we asked, the FCC said "No, the move will be in accordance to the rules this time. You must go through a 'rule-making' application."

What this meant in simple, laymen's terms was we would have to move our legal city of license from Fontana to Santa Ana, California. It should have been a fairly simple procedure, but there was just one hitch—all the other TV stations in Orange County would have to approve the move. Well, there were only two—the Coast Community College station, and Pat Boone's station in Anaheim. The college had no objection, but apparently Pat Boone did! Pat and a group of other Hollywood stars had invested in Channel 56 licensed to Anaheim, just next door to Santa Ana. Pat, along with Jimmy Durante, Fess Parker, and several other celebrities were developing Orange County's first commercial TV station.

At first, I could not understand their objections—why would Pat or his partners care if Channel 40 moved its city of license to Santa Ana? After all, we were already there operating under a temporary permit until the matter was resolved. I also pointed out that TBN was, and always would be, 100 percent Christian—certainly no threat to the commercial operations of Channel 56!

Pat presented this to his business partners, but they objected, "What if TBN ever sold Channel 40?" A new buyer could conceivably operate it as a commercial station and Pat's partners feared the competition. I pleaded with Pat, but since he was not in a majority control position, even though he was president, my pleas were denied.

Since Pat's partners were not in agreement, this opened up a very narrow and very curious rule of FCC law. Again, in simple laymen's terms, it meant we could file for the move to Santa Ana, but it also meant that ANYONE ELSE could also file for the new Santa Ana license *of OUR Channel 40!* This sounded ominous, indeed, but the alternative was either to move all of TBN out to Fontana, or up to Los Angeles. Finally, after much thought and consultation, we decided to take the chance and file for the move to Santa Ana—*a big mistake!*

Mr. Gammon had warned us that we could draw a competing application, but that our chances were good since TBN was the incumbent licensee, and we were actually on the air. What Jim Gammon did not tell me was something I would have to learn over the next five years and at the cost of over $1 million in legal fees. Follow this closely, if you've got the stomach for it, because before we are through with this chapter, it may cause you to feel as much pain as I still do over this nightmare now past. It seems there is a class of unscrupulous lawyers out there who read carefully each day the record of the FCC. When they see an application filed, they encourage a friend, or a friend of a friend, to file a competing application against it. The lawyer knows that win, lose, or draw, he gets his fee. And his client most always gets bought out by the incumbent, so he and his client all go home richer! It's a dirty business. Fortunately, the rules of the FCC have been changed to prevent most of this trafficking in TV licenses today.

I hope I'm not boring you all, but I have to lay a foundation for the absolutely unique conditions that triggered this new nightmare that was about to break upon TBN. What makes this all the more maddening, in retrospect, is the fact that new rules of the FCC now permit you to place your main studio anywhere you want under your main city grade coverage, so today we would not even have to seek FCC approval. God bless President Reagan for many of these kinds of changes and relief from government red tape!

So we filed for the move and waited the mandatory thirty days, holding our breath to see if anyone else would file for our Channel 40 license. Some of you remember along with me—
THEY DID!

It is interesting to note and remember the timing of this competing application for the license of Channel 40. In April of 1978, we had just broken through and signed our new satellite station on the air. Surely all the hosts of hell were aroused, because in less than thirty days, the very next month in May of 1978, a competing application was filed against the license of Channel 40, seeking to take it away from us for commercial purposes.

Naturally, the first thing you want to know when your TV license is filed against is: *WHO is the competitor?* We investigated and learned to our dismay that these were serious competitors made up of a group of very wealthy Orange County businessmen. One of the partners was Mr. John Virtue, who was also the president of Saddleback Broadcasting Company, our competitor. Mr. Malcomb Klein was his manager and point man, along with all the right ingredients to make for a serious threat to our Channel 40 license. *Merciful God, now what!*

TBN was beginning to expand, but Channel 40 and Southern California was still 95 percent of our support. If Channel 40 fell, that would have been the end of TBN. A panic seized my soul that I had never felt before—a sickness in the pit of my stomach that would not leave me day nor night for the next five long, agonizing years!

❧

Now the battle began in earnest. The best way to take someone's TV license away from them is to find something wrong with their operations. So our competitors visited us day after day—

inspecting our public file—taping everything we broadcast—hovering, searching, spying on everything we did.

Jan and I soon realized that we were being personally spied upon by a private detective. He followed us most everywhere we went. We actually got to know him and would wave once in a while as we left our home.

Our attorneys advised us that this was fairly routine—if they could catch either of us in some unethical or illegal activity, this would be a point against TBN, and a point in their favor as we approached the trial or hearing date to see who would receive the license of Channel 40. Other ominous events, plus anonymous phone calls, actually caused some fear for our very lives!

Finally, the other shoe fell—our competitors, in carefully examining our latest license application found, to our dismay, an inaccurate and in fact, untruthful statement in it! I had assigned the license applications to our program director, Mr. Jim Lynn, who had supervised the many functions, forms, and legwork involved in filing our license renewals. The one-foot-thick application was then forwarded to our FCC attorney for filing with the Commission.

The inaccurate statement had to do with certain dates that interviews had been conducted with community leaders, which was one of the requirements for the license application. Someone had handwritten a date of when these interviews had been conducted which, upon careful investigation by our competitors, turned out to be false.

The FCC is usually very understanding and even merciful as concerns ignorant and unintentional mistakes, but if you *EVER* lie or misrepresent anything to the FCC—look out, you will almost always be disqualified, and your license will be forfeited! Fortunately, the inaccurate statement had been, as I said, hand-written, so everyone at TBN, including myself, had to submit to a handwriting analysis expert to determine who had misrepresented the information. Oh, what agony, and the stakes were so very high. The license and the very survival of TBN were at stake.

In the meantime, depositions were ordered. Jan and I, along with many of the staff and some of our programmers, were subpoenaed to testify under oath about the various programming, engineering, and finances of TBN. It was wicked and grueling. Worst of all, we had a gag order and we could not even ask our partners to pray for us, since any mention of this battle could give TBN an unfair advantage over our competitors under FCC rules.

The darkness and despair settled in upon my soul so heavily that at times I couldn't even pray. A *Gone with the Wind*-sized novel could be written about this ordeal that seemed would never end, but neither time nor space would permit that, nor would it serve any useful purpose.

Finally, in total despair, I fell upon my office floor and told God—"Either You release me from this horror, or take me home!" I flung my Bible open, half in desperation and half in anger! My eyes fell on Jeremiah 40! Just above that very special number, these words leaped off the page at me:

*But I will deliver thee in that day, saith the LORD: and
thou shalt not be given into the hand of men of whom
thou art afraid. For I will surely deliver thee . . . because
thou hast put thy trust in me, saith the LORD. (Jeremiah
39:17–18)*

If God Himself had stepped through the wall and spoken to
me in person, He could not have said anything more comforting
or more encouraging at that moment. I was in absolute awe of the
word God had given me at my lowest point physically, mentally,
and spiritually. With that promise and assurance, I arose to face
another day and another battle.

Finally, our break came! In February of 1981, it was our turn
to depose all of the Saddleback principals and employees. As a
result, the administrative law judge granted three serious qualify-
ing issues against Saddleback! It seems they had not crossed every
"t" nor dotted every "i" either in their application.

Our attorney had taken some Saddleback depositions on a
Friday, and I had hoped to hear how they went, but Jim Gammon
never called that day. Jan and I retired that night as usual, grateful for the weekend that promised a little respite from our storm.
I could not have imagined the spiritual encounter I was to have
early the next morning.

I'm not sure if I have ever recounted this experience, but this
was perhaps the most unusual and exhilarating spiritual experience I have ever had. It must have been about daybreak, because
a faint light was just beginning to show under the thick blackout
drapes. Jan was still asleep at my side when suddenly it felt as if I

was actually rising up from my bed—*seeming to float as if lifted by the hand of God!* For a moment, I thought I must be dreaming—but no—there was Jan, there were the curtains—all the furniture and familiar surroundings were in place. Suddenly, I heard the voice of the Lord more clearly and distinctly than I ever had before—His word virtually echoed in my spirit:

THE YOKE OF THE OPPRESSOR IS BROKEN!
THE YOKE OF THE OPPRESSOR IS BROKEN!

This sentence was repeated several times as I began to feel an absolute state of euphoria! It was glorious—I was floating ever higher. *"Dear Lord, am I being translated?"*

Slowly I returned to normal as this most wonderful and exhilarating encounter faded. *What could it mean?* I wondered. *When would I know what it meant?* For some time—I can't even imagine how long—I simply lay there in the afterglow of this experience. Surely it had something to do with the Saddleback ordeal, *but what?*

When Jan awoke, I told her of this unusual encounter and together we prayed for God to reveal the meaning.

I didn't have long to wait!

❦

Early Monday morning, Jim Gammon called. He was ecstatic. "Paul, I deposed their engineer last Friday, they don't even have a transmitter site, plus there are a lot of other things in their engineering that I think completely disqualify them. I'll keep on checking and will be in touch!"

In just a few days, a call came from Saddleback's attorney—the first hint that his client would like to enter into a "settlement conference." Translation: "Pay our expenses so far and we will dismiss our competing application." Over the next several months many phone calls were exchanged, settlement offers proposed, and mountains of memos and letters exchanged. By fall we had made a deal, and on October 6, 1981, in Mr. John Virtue's office, we signed the agreement for Saddleback to DISMISS its competing application for TBN's Channel 40!

We rejoiced, but the battle was far from over. The matter of our inaccurate application and the mysterious handwriting was still an unresolved issue. The FCC designated our renewal for a hearing before an administrative law judge at the FCC—our Channel 40 license was not yet a sure thing.

We paid our competitor's costs, plus many thousands of dollars to our own attorneys; not to mention the new gray hair that had grown more apparent, nor the horrible knot in the pit of my stomach that had lasted nearly five long years.

In the next chapter I will give you the final thrill ride as we exit the Saddleback encounter forever. And I'll throw in the Merv Mattlock episode for good measure! Paul Jr. and Matt, are you still sure you want to follow old dad's footsteps into Christian TV? We'll see, won't we? The ride is far from over!

CHAPTER TWENTY-ONE

SADDLEBACK II

IN THE MIDST OF THE FINAL THROES OF THE
Saddleback affair, Jan and I were to receive another *below-the-belt
punch* that was, perhaps, the most outrageous blow of all!

I had invited Aquilla Nash, a dear sister and pastor from
Longview, Texas, to minister to our staff at TBN and to be a guest
on *Praise the Lord*. Aquilla is also, without doubt, an anointed
prophetess of the Lord who has spoken many things to me in the
Spirit. I can testify that every word she has ever given to TBN, or
to me personally, has come to pass *exactly* as prophesied.

Our prayer meeting had ended and Aquilla, Jan, and I were
walking toward my office when we passed one of our staff members in the hall. Suddenly, Aquilla stopped abruptly and asked,
"Who was that man?"

"Oh, that's Merv Mattlock, our *Praise the Lord* announcer," Jan replied.

After a long, thoughtful pause, Aquilla said, "That man is a snake in your midst and will cause you great harm! Watch out for him!"

We were shocked! *Merv, a threat to TBN?* Why, Merv had always been the gentlest, the kindest, and even the quietest young man we had on staff. I must confess that I simply did not receive Aquilla's word that day—I actually thought, *She's missed it this time*, and I really did not give the matter much more thought.

Besides, I was too busy preparing for the final hearing on our Channel 40 license at the FCC. We were forced to conduct a full-blown investigation as to who, and how, that incorrect statement got incorporated into our license application. Let me quickly say here that while I did not make the mistake, nor did I personally misrepresent anything to the Commission, I had signed the final page of the application, thereby certifying that to the best of my knowledge and belief, everything in it was true and correct. My mistake was quite simply that I had *not* read every page of the application which, as I said before, was over *ONE FOOT thick!* I had delegated that task to Jim Lynn, and other staff members, as well as to our FCC lawyers. Another BIG mistake!

With this gigantic task, along with all my regular duties—hosting *Praise the Lord,* writing the monthly newsletter, and a thousand and one other things—I was *not* prepared for the knock on my office door, nor the visit I was about to receive.

❦

Standing before me was Merv Mattlock—not too unusual, although visits such as this were fairly rare. I assumed that there must be some question about the *Praise the Lord* guest lineup for that evening. But it did not take long for me to realize that this was no ordinary visit! Merv was trembling and very obviously agitated in both spirit and body.

For a rather long and awkward moment, he just stood there saying nothing. Finally, sensing that we had a real problem here, I beckoned him to be seated over on the couch.

With quavering voice, Merv spoke. "Paul," he said, "I am here today representing a number of spiritual leaders. I have the unpleasant task . . . " His voice was now breaking with frequent throat clearing and coughing. "My task is to demand your immediate resignation as president of TBN."

At this point I did not know whether to be amused or angry. Surely this was some kind of a sick joke! But as Merv continued, I began to realize—*this was NO JOKE!*

He continued, "We have evidence that Jan is morally unfit to serve TBN, and that you have mismanaged the financial and business affairs of TBN. I have been commissioned to take charge of TBN to restore order and integrity to this ministry!" With that he handed me a letter demanding my resignation, signed by himself alone.

An 8.5 Richter scale earthquake could not have rocked me more violently! You have heard the old saying, "He was so mad he could see RED"? Let me tell you that it is not just a poetic saying—I LITERALLY SAW RED! I arose angrily and moved toward Merv, who, recognizing his folly, was now retreating rapidly through the back door of my office. Jan, hearing the commotion from the room next door, bumped headlong into Merv with me in hot pursuit! Thank God for an anointed helpmeet that day! She succeeded in restraining my fury and persuaded us to sit down and see what in heaven's name was happening. Merv was now violently shaking as he nervously eyed me.

The details of the accusations I will not even dignify by mentioning. Every one eventually proved to be absolutely false as we submitted them to our board and elders. "So, who are these *SPIRITUAL LEADERS* that you represent?" Jan demanded!

Merv would identify only one—*John Wesley Fletcher*—who was back at Heritage USA in Charlotte, North Carolina. I immediately picked up the phone and got right through to John. When confronted by the allegations and his participation in Merv Mattlock's *coup d'état,* he categorically denied any knowledge of, or participation in, Merv's insane demands. Finally, after Merv refused to name any of the *other* "spiritual leaders" who had commissioned him to confront me, I turned to Merv once more, telling him that he had ten minutes to clean out his desk and remove himself from the premises of TBN!

To this day, I am not sure just what, or who, prompted this unspeakable attack on Jan and me—I will never believe that Merv was acting solely on his own. And now, we will probably never know because, well, there is yet one amusing and one tragic episode to the Merv Mattlock affair. We'll deal with that in a succeeding chapter.

❧

By now, we were nearing the trial date of our FCC hearing. Remember, the license of Channel 40 was still on the line. The false statement, in simple terms, certified that certain community leadership interviews had been conducted in a certain month, when indeed they had not been. The burning question was, *Whose mysterious handwriting was it on the application?* Jim Lynn, who had supervised the application, steadfastly denied it was his! The two secretaries who assisted Jim also denied any culpability. *So who?*

Also, to mystify the whole matter even more, this page in question had been cut mysteriously and a new portion Scotch-taped over the original section! Oh, how I wished I had read and wept over each and every page! *Could some enemy have doctored our application?* I wondered.

The handwriting expert finally issued his findings—the handwriting, he believed, was Jim Lynn's; but Jim still declared, under oath, that he had no recollection whatsoever of writing this false statement on our application.

Ultimately, it was my time to take the witness stand. I was sworn in and the questioning began. The FCC prosecutors were merciless—*"Did you realize that by signing the application you were certifying that everything in it was true and correct?"*

"Yes" was my unqualified answer.

"Didn't you realize that it was your responsibility to assure yourself that every page was, indeed, true and correct?"

My response was, "I thought I had, by assigning the task to my senior staff members, as well as to our FCC attorneys."

Finally, the question that I knew would ultimately come: *"Did you, Paul F. Crouch, KNOW that this incorrect and untrue statement was contained in the application at the time you had signed it?"*

Throughout all of the hearing and testimony I had held my small Bible in my hand, or had it within reach at all times. Ignoring the attorneys who had mercilessly grilled me all afternoon, I turned to the judge on his bench and said, "Your honor, I respect the authority of this court, and the pursuit of truth and justice for which it stands. But your honor," I continued, "I also answer to a higher court and Judge who is the Author of this Book I hold in my hand." With that, I laid my Bible out on the table at my side and placed my hand squarely upon it.

"Your honor," I concluded, "I swear by Almighty God that I did not know that there was a false and inaccurate statement in the application in question."

The judge and I maintained total eye contact as I answered the final question as truthfully as I knew how before God and man. I could see it immediately in the judge's eyes—*he believed me*—I knew this nightmare was nearing an end!

Even so, the wheels of justice move exceedingly slow at the FCC. The original hearing order had been issued in October of 1980. We had signed our release with Saddleback in October of 1981. I had given testimony in July of 1982, but the final decision of Judge Thomas B. Fitzpatrick was not released until January 17, 1983.

In his "Ultimate Findings of Fact and Conclusion of Law," Judge Fitzpatrick wrote, among many other things, the following:

It is concluded that TBN is not disqualified to be a licensee and that the public interest would be served by a grant of its application.

In another paragraph the judge continued:

The record establishes that Crouch was unaware when he signed the application that it contained a misrepresentation . . . As a consequence, Crouch is innocent of any misrepresentation or wrongdoing.

And finally, the most blessed line of all in conclusion:

Accordingly, it is ordered, that . . . the construction permit application of TBN, Inc. is GRANTED.

The decision was released to the public record on January 25, 1983, and it became final fifty days later on March 16, 1983! The nightmare had ended—the morning had come! We were free to remain in Orange County, with a waiver to keep our main studios in the suburb of Tustin, California, right next door to Santa Ana, California, our NEW city of license.

But there is a most interesting and blessed postscript to the whole Saddleback affair. You will remember that John Virtue, a prominent Orange County attorney, had been the president of this group that had tried desperately to take the license of Channel 40 from us. It was at least three or four years after the conclusion of the Saddleback chapter that I received a personal call from none other than John Virtue.

"Paul," he said, "I just wanted to call and tell you that your guest on *Praise the Lord* last night really got to me!"

For a moment I had to think—*ah, yes*—another lawyer, Gene Neill, the Miami "lawyer criminal" who had been sentenced to fifty years in federal prison.

Mr. Virtue continued, "I also want to say how personally sorry I am for all of the pain we surely caused you."

I assured John of our unconditional forgiveness, that as believers in Jesus Christ, we were commanded to forgive, and that I hoped he had found his peace with God.

He assured me that he had and, in conclusion, he asked me to convey his thanks and best wishes to his fellow lawyer, Gene Neill, who had been saved in federal prison and then released from his fifty-year sentence by a miracle of God. We concluded in wishing each other well as we continued our mutual lives and futures.

My children, remember this truth and Scripture well, for it is an important key to your future blessings and success:

> *When a man's ways please the* LORD, *he maketh even his enemies to be at peace with him. (Proverbs 16:7)*

We move now quickly, yes, to the next battle in this thirty-year odyssey of TBN.

CHAPTER TWENTY-TWO

JOSEPH'S BRETHREN—THE NRB

AFTER THE SADDLEBACK ORDEAL I HOPED, I PRAYED, that God would give us a respite from the ceaseless and merciless attacks that had besieged us, it seemed, from the first day that God had spoken to Jan and me and called us to this incredible theater of spiritual warfare. Actually, God did, and for the next several years, TBN entered into the most awesome period of spiritual and numerical growth we had experienced to date.

President Reagan declared 1983 "THE YEAR OF THE BIBLE" and we joined joyfully with Dr. Bill Bright and many other evangelical leaders in highlighting the Word of God and calling for its renewal at home, in our churches, and in our institutions of higher learning. The ACLU filed suit, but before the courts could even consider the matter, 1983 had ended. We had celebrated "THE YEAR OF THE BIBLE" and our opposition's objections were moot and outdated.

The next few years were years of unprecedented growth and victories. As I have commented so often: the first decade of TBN produced *three* TV stations; the second decade produced more than *4,000* TV stations. The third decade took our breath away with more than *three thousand* stations, as we shall soon see! Looking back, I can see clearly why Satan tried desperately to destroy us in the early stages—he knew we were on the threshold of the most explosive communications growth in the history of the Christian church. He knew that *GOD'S NETWORK* was poised to invade his cherished strongholds: *THE AIRWAVES!* As I have reminded the evil one so often—he is only *TEMPORARILY* the "prince of the power of the air." He must and WILL yield his dominion of the airwaves, as *GOD'S TV NETWORK* pierces his cherished domain!

For the next several years, TV stations flashed ON THE AIR in unprecedented numbers. Affiliate stations joined the TBN network; low-power or full-power stations signed on the air at an average of one a week! Cable stations joined so fast, we could not even count them!

Our one *"HOLY BEAMER"* mobile satellite truck, which TBN pioneered in the late 1970s, now became four "holy beamers" crisscrossing the nation, bringing the great spiritual events of the Body of Christ—*LIVE*—into millions of homes across America.

Then, *wonder of wonders,* foreign nations began opening up to Christian TV! Our first station on foreign soil was Nevis-St. Christopher in the eastern Caribbean islands, followed by stations in El Salvador, Belize, Guatemala, Italy, and South Africa. Chinese *Praise the Lord,* Haitian *Praise the Lord,* and Indonesian *Praise the Lord* swelled the airwaves with the glory of the Lord! It seemed we were *finally free*—on our way to preach *"THIS GOSPEL"* to every creature!

☙

But in 1987—*wham! It hit!* First the PTL scandal, followed by the Jimmy Swaggart revelations, and to a lesser degree many others were also drawn into the TV EVANGELIST SCANDAL era. TBN was able to remain largely above the fray, but the fallout was universal. Every Christian ministry in the nation was affected to some degree. For months, even years, the failures of a few dominated the secular and even the religious news.

It seemed that every institution in the land followed suit, with the savings and loans scandals, the stock-market scandals—even the Congressional banking scandals. In more recent years it was the corporate scandals—Enron, Worldcom, and other lesser lights. The secular media, and especially the tabloid papers, had their scandal heyday as obscure names all the way to world-famous names met their day of reckoning, had their day in court, and some went to prison for varying crimes and terms. Events of the late 1980s brought to mind the warning of the Apostle Paul, who wrote:

> *Yet once more I shake not the earth only, but also heaven . . . that those things which cannot be shaken may remain. (Hebrews 12:26–27)*

TBN had already been "shaken" so many times we had lost count, but there was to be yet another shaking!

This time it was directed at me personally, and it broke in January of 1988 as I registered for the National Religious Broadcasters convention in Washington, D.C. I had been a member and a supporter of NRB for many years, attending and participating in its many worthwhile and interesting activities. For one thing, the Commissioners of the FCC always spoke to us, giving us the latest in the rules and regulations, which was invaluable to broadcasters. Most years the president of the United States came and addressed the members, offering encouragement and admonition to us in the religious broadcasting field.

It was also a time of fellowship and learning, as we attended and participated in the many workshops and conferences, culminating always in a great awards banquet, where various broadcasters and station owners were honored for years of service and special achievements.

I was especially excited because TBN was to be honored this year as the outstanding foreign broadcaster of the year in recognition of our new foreign stations coming on-line. But as I registered, several friends and acquaintances came to me privately and said, "Paul, we hear that Paul Roper is calling a news conference tomorrow to charge you with moral failures. We understand that two women will testify of various affairs with YOU!"

I was stunned and sickened by what I knew was a lie of the lowest sort. But Paul Roper had gained national notoriety in the Jim

Bakker scandal, and just the mention of his name seemed to add credibility to the rumor.

The morning came with no press conference or announcement. I called Mr. Colby May, our FCC attorney, and asked him to confer with me. I also called Mr. Philip Little, a private investigator, who had helped us with numerous other difficulties, and asked him to fly to Washington immediately for consultation.

The next day I was summoned to the room of Dr. Thomas Zimmerman, one of the executive board members of NRB. Dr. Zimmerman was also the General Superintendent of the Assemblies of God and had been my pastor in Springfield, Missouri, during most of my growing-up years. He had also baptized me in water as I gave my public confession of faith at twelve years of age.

The news he gave me was ominous. "Paul," he said, "the brethren have heard that moral allegations are going to be brought against you, and we have decided that the award that was to be presented to you tomorrow night should be withheld until this matter is cleared up."

Now I was incensed! "Brother Zimmerman," I said, "this rumor has not a shred of truth to it, and I demand a meeting with the *'BRETHREN'* who have made this decision without so much as one word of inquiry to me!"

Brother Zimmerman was sympathetic and agreed to call a meeting of the full board of the NRB the next afternoon. Within twenty-four hours, I had my meeting, flanked by my FCC attorney and my private investigator. I demanded to hear their evidence or to meet my accusers. To my dismay, I learned that the decision to withhold the TBN award that night was based on pure rumor and hearsay! Not one witness—not one fact—could be presented.

Finally, after much discussion, I reached for my Bible. Laying my hand upon it, I said, "Gentlemen, I swear by Almighty God, at the peril of my eternal soul burning in hell, that I have never touched a woman other than my wife, in a sexual way, either before or after marriage!"

For several moments the several board members sat in stunned silence. Finally, Dr. Robert Cook, president of NRB, spoke. "Paul, we owe you an apology. Will you stay and let us honor you with the broadcaster award as planned?" When he saw I was struggling with the decision, he continued. "Let us apologize to you BIG, tonight!"

Frankly, I was ready to shake the dust off my feet on the NRB; in fact, I had already called my pilot and ordered him to warm up the engines on Eagle I! But Bob Cook, great statesman that he was, won the day. That night, I sat at a place of honor next to my former pastor, Dr. Thomas Zimmerman, and TBN was honored as scheduled with the Foreign Broadcaster of the Year award.

The rumors were laid to rest, and since Paul Roper vehemently denied any knowledge or complicity with this attack, it remains a mystery to this day as to who originated this reprehensible lie.

So now my honor was restored, my good name reinstated in the honor roll of the NRB, *right?* Guess again, children. Round two is coming up. It's about to get really nasty this time! Want to hear more? Read on, if you have the stomach for it!

CHAPTER TWENTY-THREE

TO NRB, OR NOT TO NRB

YOU WOULD THINK BY NOW THAT JAN AND I should have developed hides as thick as rhinoceroses', but as I told you earlier, when the wounds come from your *"brothers"* in Christ—the pain is indescribable!

But before going any further, let's put all modern-day Christian suffering into proper perspective. Compared to what Jesus suffered for us—well, none of us have *really* suffered very much, have we? Also, compared to many of the early disciples and followers of Christ, we have also suffered very little. Read *Foxe's Book of Martyrs* and we must all hang our heads in shame for ever complaining about any suffering or hardship for following Jesus.

In some ways, however, the assassination of your good name and character can be just as—if not more—painful than a physical

173

execution. At least if they kill you physically you are instantly with Christ! On the other hand, vicious lies and rumors, and attacks aimed at the very heart of your character protract the pain and suffering over many months and even years.

Such was the case with this second-wave assault—this time from the *"Ethics Committee"* of the National Religious Broadcasters.

It all started in late January of 1989. Jan and I had missed the NRB convention that year, having scheduled a series of TBN live *Praise the Lord* programs beginning in Phoenix, Arizona. We were *"having church"* at Pastor Don Price's great Valley Cathedral. A spiritual breakthrough had come, and well over 1,000 phoned in one night to receive Christ—it was glorious! Remember in my introduction I spoke of a night that I threw a thousand salvation slips into the air in ecstasy as partners rejoiced from coast to coast? Well, this was the time of that great spiritual revival.

I suppose we should have braced ourselves—it always seems that an all-out satanic attack comes on the heels of great spiritual breakthroughs. On the other hand, these dark valleys and spiritual assaults from the evil one usually signals a great spiritual or physical VICTORY up ahead as well!

My children, beware if there are no spiritual battles in your lives and ministries. As much as we do dread them, they are most always the proof that we are accomplishing something for God— that we are damaging the kingdom of darkness. If you don't "mess" with the devil, he usually won't "mess" with you! Well, by 1989 we had just passed the 100 TV-station mark, so we were *messing* with the devil for sure!

🐚

Well, the second NRB bombshell landed January 31, 1989, with a call from Mark Pinsky, a reporter for the *Los Angeles Times*. He stated to my secretary, Margie Tuccillo, that he had a copy of a complaint that had been filed with the NRB Ethics Committee against TBN and Paul Crouch. When Margie asked for details about this "complaint," he refused any further comment, demanding to speak only to Paul Crouch. He did say that his deadline was Wednesday and that a major article would break in the February 2 issue of the *Times*.

And BREAK it did! Without warning or any contact whatsoever from the NRB, the Thursday morning, February 2, 1989, issue of the *L.A. Times* read: "ETHICS PANEL INVESTIGATING CROUCH, TBN." We learned later that the same story broke in several other papers across the States, primarily in cities where TBN had major TV stations. The article began as follows:

> Paul F. Crouch, founder and president of Tustin-based Trinity Broadcasting Network, is under investigation by the ethics committee of the National Religious Broadcasters, committee chairman Richard Bott Sr. has confirmed.

The *Times* article continued:

> Bott, who was interviewed before the NRB convention, declined to provide details. But according to a 17-page

complaint submitted to the ethics committee—copies of which have been given to *The Times* . . ."

Of course, Mr. Bott did not need to provide details of the charges—the *Times* reporter had been furnished with a complete copy of the complaint! Naturally, Mr. Pinsky refused to reveal his "UNNAMED SOURCES," and it remains a mystery to this day as to just *who* gave a copy of this complaint to the *Times*, but here is the *ZINGER!*

The *L.A. Times* article appeared, as I said, on February 2. The letter from Mr. Bott of the NRB, which gave TBN its first glimpse of the charges, was dated *FEBRUARY 8!*

The *Times* article continued:

> The complaint against Crouch was filed by the Rev. Heath Kaiser of Dallas. In a telephone interview . . . Kaiser said he has been battling Crouch in the courts and before the Federal Communications Commission for . . . control of WTBY-TV Channel 54, in Poughkeepsie, New York.

It is interesting to note that later in the same article Kaiser himself admitted:

> There is no action pending before the FCC which has granted a license for Channel 54 to Trinity without reservation.

When the documents relating to the purchase of the New York station were examined and the truth revealed, it became abundantly clear that TBN had purchased Channel 54 from Mr. Kaiser and his several partners in complete compliance with all of the terms and conditions of the agreement. Trinity not only paid the full contract price—in excess of $3 million dollars—for a TV station that was totally insolvent and on the verge of bankruptcy, but as a gesture of goodwill and compassion, after the contract was signed, we agreed voluntarily to add an extra 16 percent above and beyond the agreed purchase price of the stock. We provided this additional consideration to aid each shareholder, including Mr. Kaiser, for extra legal and accounting expenses they had incurred. We felt this was a generous act on our part, but our reward was to become embroiled in a complicated and pro-tracted lawsuit that lasted more than seven years.

Not only had Mr. Kaiser participated in this lawsuit against TBN, but had also assisted and encouraged other former employees of Channel 54 to file complaints with the FCC, culminating in Mr. Kaiser's own petition to the FCC that sought the denial of our scheduled license renewal. This prompted a full-scale field investigation by the staff of the FCC, which resulted in WTBY-TV Channel 54's uncondi-tional renewal of its station license. The FCC found Mr. Kaiser's charges and complaints to be totally without merit! Even after the FCC had ruled in our favor, Mr. Kaiser still filed these same charges with the NRB that he knew had been dis-missed by the FCC!

Additional charges in the NRB complaint included the fact that TBN had built new Christian TV stations in areas or near areas where existing Christian TV stations were operating. This was true, but my response was and is that *ALL TV stations ought to be CHRISTIAN!* Other Christian operators have built second and even third Christian stations in cities where TBN has stations without any protest on our part. *I praise God for every one!* There is hardly a major market in the nation that does not have one or more Christian radio stations—why should there be a limit on TV stations? Each station and operator brings a unique and needed emphasis to the viewer, so I still declare—*build MORE Christian TV and radio stations!* If we are all moving in the will of God, HE will bless and provide for all!

Another charge was an outright misrepresentation. It was alleged that when TBN purchased Channel 21 in Phoenix, Arizona, as I explained earlier, we had assumed over $2 million dollars in bond indebtedness that was in default. We had assumed this debt, but the misrepresentation alleged that TBN had defaulted by offering the bondholders a tax-deductible receipt in lieu of the cash they were entitled to! The record here was and is clear—except for a few who had voluntarily donated their bonds, TBN, through its sister corporation, Trinity of Arizona, PAID EACH AND EVERY BONDHOLDER IN FULL, *two years ahead* of the agreed-upon schedule of redemption!

I could write another book on other baseless charges that I will not even dignify by detailing them here. I could add other chapters telling of Mr. Kaiser's many other attempts to stop our addition of new TV stations in Seattle, Canton-Akron, and even our initial efforts in South Africa. It seemed for a time that every application we filed at the FCC was met by some objection or petition to deny filed by Mr. Kaiser! All of Mr. Kaiser's filings were overruled or found to be meritless by the FCC but, of course, these actions needlessly drained resources and energies from TBN and the Kingdom of God.

☜

We learned later that *SOMEONE* had also distributed copies of this seventeen-page confidential complaint throughout the entire constituency of the NRB! When we requested a copy of the procedures that the NRB Ethics Committee would be following in this investigation, we received no reply! We realized, finally, that we were being thrust into a form of litigation without even knowing what the ground rules were!

Finally, eight days after the news of these charges was plastered all over the front pages of newspapers from coast to coast, we received our letter from Mr. Richard Bott, chairman of the Ethics Committee of the NRB. Enclosed was the seventeen-page complaint signed, under oath, by Heath Kaiser. We were given thirty days to respond to the charges.

I immediately responded with a letter to Mr. Bott, demanding a face-to-face meeting with my accuser, at which I agreed to provide complete documentation as to the falsity and absurdity of the allegations. My request was never even responded to!

For days my attorneys and I prepared our eleven-page detailed response, proving with voluminous documentation and exhibits the falsity of each charge. Stacks of sworn affidavits, reams of official records from the files of the FCC, decisions of other governmental agencies and courts of law were assembled for presentation.

By the time we had finished our work, the letter and exhibits were several inches thick!

But before we could complete our work on the first attack, the second bombshell landed! Mr. Bott's second letter enclosed another list of complaints, this time from our old nemesis Merv Mattlock. It was basically a rehash of his earlier financial and moral charges, the ones he leveled at me when he had marched into my office demanding my resignation as president of TBN.

Naturally, this second charge made its rounds through the news media with new stories of gruesome details of how cruel Jan and I were to all our employees! Every single charge was either an outright lie or a half-truth that led to an absolutely false conclusion. Again, I will not dignify these accusations by responding to them, nor waste good time and paper reciting his totally unsubstantiated rumors, but a little comic relief is needed about here!

❧

When Merv had left us rather abruptly after his unfounded accusations, he moved to Tulsa, Oklahoma, to work with Kenneth Hagin Ministries. The word had circulated back through the TBN staff that Merv was now *"in charge"* of all Hagin TV and radio ministries, a much better and more responsible job than he previously held as *Praise the Lord* announcer at TBN.

But I will never forget the night that "Dad" Hagin had driven over from Tulsa to Oklahoma City to be our special guest on *Praise the Lord*. I did not know until after the program that Merv had driven Dad along with his son, Ken Hagin Jr., to the studio that night. Shortly before the program was to begin I walked into the men's rest room only to behold a sight that shall forever be etched into the recesses of my memory. It is one I shall also cherish as long as I live.

There at the washbasin stood Dr. Kenneth Hagin in his stocking feet with red Oklahoma mud caked up to his knees! There on the Pullman sat his beautiful new cowboy boots with Ken Hagin Jr. feverishly wiping the sticky clay from them as the *Praise the Lord* theme echoed down the halls of Channel 14! The problem had been caused by our parking-lot repaving project. Only half of the asphalt had been laid—the other half was "Oklahoma red" and it had just rained. Dad's car had been parked on the edge of the new parking lot and as he got out—well, you can guess the rest!

Needless to say, we did not take any leg shots of Dad that night—nor even any long shots for that matter. But all in all, Dad was a good sport and we all pitched in to get him cleaned up enough for the program. Dad was vintage Hagin that night as he taught us the word of FAITH as only he can. The viewers never knew that Dad's feet were planted firmly in material that looked more like red brick by the end of the three-hour program.

As fate would have it, Dad, Ken Jr., Merv, and I all bumped into each other at the corner of two halls as Dad was leaving for home. Ken Jr. called out to Merv in his inimitable Oklahoma drawl, *"Go git the ker, Merv—and this time don't park her in the mud so that Diddy gits his feet muddy!"* Merv exited hastily amid peals of laughter from several TBN staffers who were within earshot.

This phrase—*"Go git the ker"*—has since been immortalized by the staff of TBN and has been broadened, mainly by the engineers, as requests are issued to *"go git"* most anything from a pencil to a "Holy Beamer."

Sadly, Merv's tenure at the Hagin Ministries did not last long, and we learned that he had moved from job to job, finally deciding to start a secular singing career. When that did not prove successful he finally called and persuaded me to meet him for lunch. At that meeting, Merv requested that I consider rehiring him for a position back at TBN. I explained that while none of us at TBN held any ill will toward him, and had unconditionally forgiven him for his previous attacks, there would never be another job for him at TBN.

When I made this abundantly clear, Merv's attitude changed dramatically and he advised me that he would now take his story to the secular media—*60 Minutes, 20/20,* or one of several exposé-type TV shows. He also threatened to write a book which, in his NRB letter, he said would be titled *Godfathers of the Gospel.*

I told Merv, as we parted for the last time on this earth, that I still loved him and forgave him for all of his anger and seeming hatred of TBN and me.

Merv's exposé was never made nor was his book written. A few months after his final attack through the NRB, Merv died of cancer at forty-six years of age. All we could do was the same we had done for Ward Vanguard—commit him into the hands of a loving and merciful Lord and move on.

❦

The final round of allegations to the NRB turned into a veritable insane asylum! New charges came from Ray Wilson, better known as "Black Buffalo," producer of a children's TV program.

Fifteen-year-old charges were dredged up from my days of employment at Faith Center, including a number of false allegations that ranged from stealing the church mailing list to cheating widows and orphans out of their life savings! All of this had been disproved and laid to rest years ago, but here came the charges again, *and all carefully timed and leaked to the news media to gain maximum exposure!*

I called Jerry Rose, who was then president of NRB. I pled with him to order the face-to-face meeting that I had demanded by letter to Richard Bott so that we could settle this uproar as brothers in Christ, but to no avail. The sad truth: TBN was put on TRIAL by my Christian brothers through carefully timed and expertly orchestrated leaks, interviews, and releases to *the secular media!*

I still grieve for a lost and dying world whose only glimpse of Jesus was a Christian lynching party out to get one of their own brothers! My numerous pleas for a face-to-face meeting with my accusers was first ignored and finally turned down. My pleas to follow the scriptural mandate were denied:

> *Brethren, if a man be overtaken in a fault, ye which are spiritual, restore such an one in the spirit of meekness; considering thyself, lest thou also be tempted. (Galatians 6:1)*

In the depths of this maelstrom of charges, countercharges, lies, and scandalous media reports, a word of wisdom came to me from my angel, Jan. It was written in her own hand. It was folded neatly and lying on my Bible where she knew I would find it the next morning at my prayer time.

Paul, God chose you to carry the cross of being hurt in the press so that others who go through this can be ministered to by *you!*

God looked all over His world and found someone that would go through this trial and would not get discouraged or give up! God loved you so much, He trusted *you* with this and knew you would not "blow it" for Him.

If I can, you can!

I love you—Jan

I can tell you that Jan's word of encouragement just may have made the difference for me at a very critical moment in my life. I will be forever grateful to her obedience to the Holy Spirit. It is also at times like these that your love for each other grows stronger and deeper than ever.

Finally, after nearly two years of charges, countercharges, rumors, and exhaustive investigation and examination of mountains of documents, the NRB Executive Committee issued this terse statement in December of 1991:

After reviewing the materials made available to it, the Committee finds there is insufficient evidence to warrant termination of membership.

I immediately tendered my resignation to the NRB, which prompted another whole round of media stories and speculations.

Well, there you have it—one of the saddest chapters in the life of TBN, mostly because of the sick and twisted perception that the world received from CHRISTIANS! I am sure that as a result, many turned a deaf ear to our message—I pray none will be lost from Christ because of these scandalous attacks against TBN and me. I know that my responses were uttered in defense of the truth as I saw and understood it.

And yet there is a brighter ending to this chapter than you might expect. First of all, there are MANY good and godly members of the NRB. Most are still my dear friends and brothers in Christ. The rest I have forgiven and hold no bitterness toward—may God be my witness.

Remember, my children, unforgiveness and bitterness only hurt the one who holds on to it. The one you are bitter against may not even be aware of *your* problem. Besides, forgiveness is NOT an option if you choose to be a true follower of Jesus Christ. He Himself said:

> *For if ye forgive men their trespasses, your heavenly Father will also forgive you: But if ye forgive not men their trespasses, neither will your Father forgive your trespasses. (Matthew 6:14–15)*

I know, in the natural, that it is difficult most of the time to forgive those who have hurt you, but just remember this: forgiveness is simply a choice—I choose to forgive and when I do, something wonderful happens—suddenly I AM FREE! There is even a medical dimension to unforgiveness and bitterness, as Dr.

Donald Whitaker and Dr. Reginald Cherry and others have taught us. It literally creates a physical and chemical imbalance that contributes to a whole host of other physical ailments from ulcers to cancer! So learn this lesson well, my children—*FORGIVE*—there are NO options. Finally, when you make the decision to forgive—God ALWAYS gives you the ability to release the hurt, the pain, or the grief to Him!

Another positive aspect to this whole ordeal might be drawn from the fact that nearly two years of digging and investigation of TBN turned up *"INSUFFICIENT EVIDENCE TO WARRANT TERMINATION OF MEMBERSHIP."* Pretty high praise, I'd say—how about you? Another very interesting byline to this point came from another former enemy. Do you remember Mr. John Virtue of our Saddleback chapter? During the NRB's time of probing for scandal about TBN and me, a prominent newspaper reporter called Mr. Virtue, knowing that he and his group had probed earlier for nearly five years into the very heart of TBN. Mr. Virtue sent me a copy of a letter that he wrote to the editor of the *Los Angeles Times*. In his letter he recounted the conversation in which he informed a very disappointed newspaper reporter that he should give up on his search for dirt concerning TBN and me. Mr. Virtue's letter speaks for itself and included the following:

> I read with disappointment your recent article concerning Paul Crouch, and his activities in Christian broadcasting.
>
> My impression is that your reporter entered into an investigation hoping to find material of a damaging

nature, on the order of the recent scandals involving other Christian broadcasters.

I was interviewed by your reporter in connection with the article, and my impression of your negative approach arose because of the nature of the questions, which were essentially a search for material damaging to Mr. Crouch.

The reason for my interview was, that for several years, I headed a group that filed a challenge with the Federal Communications Commission to the license of the Santa Ana television station owned by the Paul Crouch broadcasting group. During that time, in connection with our challenge, we made an investigation, and searched for background information, that would be damaging to Mr. Crouch or his organization. We found no negative information, only positive information.

I informed your reporter of this, and further informed him that during our license challenge, Mr. Crouch was at all times a gentleman, polite, and sincere in his beliefs. The reporter told me that he had heard this from other parties he had interviewed.

My disappointment with your article is that as I read it, I looked for some positive results from the investigation, but only found the negatives.

The article, although not materially damaging either to Mr. Crouch or his activities, raised doubts because the *Times* printed it in a nonobjective manner, and many readers, hoping to find negative news about Christian broadcasting, found solace in the fact that it was printed in this fashion.

I thanked Mr. Virtue most heartily for this good report and also for letting me know of it.

And finally, Jan and I even accepted formal Christian conciliation with Heath Kaiser, who had participated in the whole NRB ordeal. The result was total and unconditional forgiveness and release of all bitterness and claims toward each other for the past. But of course, that never made the papers or any of the secular media.

By the way, I still hold out the hand of fellowship to the NRB just as Joseph did to his brothers!

So, is there life after NRB? Surely this would be the final test. From here on, after such exoneration, surely God would give us a break and allow us to get down to business—the explosive growth and expansion of the network.

Ah, children, I told you earlier that the deeper you go in God—the deeper you drive into enemy territory. It does not get easier—it gets harder! But like the great Apostle Paul, we learn "HIS GRACE IS SUFFICIENT." In the chapters that follow, Jan and I found unknown new depths of suffering, disappointment, and sorrow. Yet "THROUGH IT ALL," we found new heights of God's strength and deliverance. This old hymn—*He Giveth More Grace*—took on new meaning and comfort:

> *He giveth more grace*
> *When the burdens grow greater.*

He sendeth more strength
When the labors increase.
To added afflictions, he addeth His mercy.
To multiplied trials, His multiplied peace.
His love hath no limits, His grace hath no measure.
His power hath no boundary known unto man.
For out of His infinite riches in Jesus,
He giveth, and giveth, and giveth again.

Brace yourselves, children, we are headed for the gates of hell!

CHAPTER TWENTY-FOUR

ON OUR WAY TO THE GATES OF HELL

SO, HOW DO YOU DESCRIBE THE "GATES OF HELL"? I have heard many a barn-burner sermon on the horrors of hell, *"where their worm dieth not, and the fire is not quenched"* (Mark 9:44)! I have heard the testimony of some who have had near-death experiences and have returned to warn all to escape that place of torment. Of course, nothing we can experience in this life can really compare to an eternity lost from the presence of God, but when you are going through your fiery trials, deep waters, or shadow of death, it seems the only way to express it is to say, "I'm going through hell!"

You might say, "Why, Paul? Why take us through *your* hell? We have enough of our own hell on earth—we don't need any of yours."

Well, my children, believe me, it would be a lot easier for me to try and forget this next ordeal, but I want you to know that in your darkest hours—and they will come—that we really do have a faith that works! I want this chapter to be a testimony of encouragement that you and others may take strength and comfort from when you are there.

I can remember the nights—how I dreaded nights—when it seemed hopeless. Alone much of the time, I literally felt trapped in a prison with no way out. I did struggle for a time as to whether or not I should open my heart and share with you the new depths to which this chapter in the history of TBN has taken us, but then I read in 2 Corinthians 11 how the Apostle Paul opened his heart to the church of his day and shared the depths to which his journey had taken him.

Let me hasten to say that I do not compare the depths of our suffering with his—God forbid! Who among us has been stoned three times? I have not suffered shipwreck. I have not been "beaten with rods" or received thirty-nine stripes, five times!

And yet, there are some similarities. *"In journeyings often"*— yes! *"In perils of robbers"*—yes! Today, crafty lawyers file scurrilous petitions at the FCC to extort huge sums of money from us! *"In perils by mine own countrymen"*—yes! *"In perils in the city and wilderness"*—yes! *"In perils among false brethren"*—yes, yes, yes!

So why does the great apostle take us through this long litany of his trials and tribulations? Well, maybe in part just to "get it off his chest," as we say. But the real reason is given in verse 30:

> *If I must needs glory, I will glory in the things which concern my infirmities. (2 Corinthians 11:30)*

In other words, even though we get the daylights beaten out of us, the GOOD NEWS continues to go around the world and, even better, Jesus gets all the praise and credit in spite of human weakness!

❦

While the suffering of Paul's day is very different from ours—we do not receive literally the sting of a whip—yet the inner stripes and the emotional suffering are very real, as all of us can testify. But before I open the gate, let me give you this word of encouragement: in those darkest hours God always met me. When those "fiery darts" would hit and it felt like my heart and whole inner being was falling out, it was like—and this is hard to explain—God built a steel girder under the pit of my stomach, holding everything in place!

The old country song is all wrong—believe me—only God can "help you make it through the night"! And yes, just as the Word says, there are indeed "songs in the night"! Just know that when you are in the will of God, and if your cause is right, you can't lose! Remember this—you, too, will need it!

So, when and how did this nightmare begin? Buckle up and hunker down—this ride is a real roller coaster!

CHAPTER TWENTY-FIVE

HELL IS AROUSED

IT WAS 1990. I HAD JUST RETURNED FROM MY FIRST trip to Russia where I had met with the mayor of the city Leningrad (later changed to St. Petersburg) to explore the possibility of a Christian TV station there. I had been warmly received and given good encouragement and even instruction on the political situation and how to make the application.

We went to work immediately—formed the corporation and filed the application. In 1991 Jan and I returned with a group of about two hundred partners to St. Petersburg, Moscow, and Kiev for three exciting evangelistic crusades.

It is interesting to remember that the Soviet Union and communism had just collapsed. The nation was in great turmoil and distress. The people were wide open to the Gospel! We rented the big Olympic auditorium and had the joy of introducing a new generation of Russian youth to Jesus Christ! Jan and I were amazed by the response from people who had been taught for more than seventy years that there was no God!

We rejoiced as the Power Team of strong, young athletes broke bricks, ice, and handcuffs to the delight of everyone. Jeff Fenholt told of his deliverance from drugs and salvation through Christ. The audiences seemed to know Jeff from the Black Sabbath rock group, and his old Broadway days of *Jesus Christ Superstar*. Now Jeff introduced them to the real Jesus Christ!

Dino brought them to their feet with great piano classics by Russian composers, and to our amazement they seemed to know some of the old hymns he played! Jan and I shared the miracle of all Christian television in America and told of our dream for it in Russia. During this visit I met with Mr. Anatoly Sobchak, who had become the new mayor of St. Petersburg. Mr. Sobchak gave us great encouragement and support to build Russia's first Christian TV station.

I could write a whole book on the three years in a row we went to Russia, and the miracle of that first station that signed on the air in 1993. Those dear partners who went with us will remember how nearly every hand was raised as the invitation was given to receive Christ! I was so shocked, I asked the interpreter to repeat the question: "How many for the very first time are receiving Jesus Christ?" Same response—virtually every hand went up again. I suppose we should not have been surprised given seventy years of atheism!

❦

One amazing story I must tell before going on happened on that second trip to St. Petersburg right on the eve of the collapse of communism. We were returning from the mayor's office to the airport when I spied a huge statue of Lenin. It was in the middle of a football-field-sized plaza, in front of a large, gray, government building. I asked the driver to stop so Jan and I, along with our attorney, Norm Juggert, could take a picture. My son Matt was our cameraman, along with his wife, Lori, and our grandson, Caylan.

It is tough not to stop here and tell how Caylan—then about eighteen months old—had made a hit with everyone in the mayor's office. The secretaries especially went nuts over him, and I can still see him crawling around on the floor of his honor, the mayor's grand office! Caylan just may be the reason we got that first TV station license!

Anyway, as we posed under the giant statue, a beautiful lady appeared, seemingly out of nowhere, and walked up to Jan. She was dressed in a beautiful flowing robe and had a long-stemmed pink rose in her hand. With a smile she extended the rose to Jan and in perfect English said, *"Thank you—thank you."* By then Matt was putting the camera back in the car, so I called to him to bring it back for a picture of this lovely lady. But as I turned to ask the lady to pose with us—*she had vanished from our sight!* There were no trees or other vegetation, and the plaza was a hundred yards in all directions.

For several minutes we all stood in shock and amazement! Surely this was an angel—at least a heavenly visitor! Jan actually saw her two more times on later trips to Russia—both in the Moscow airport. She never spoke a word, but on the last visit, after the first TV station was on the air, she looked at Jan and gave her my old "thumbs-up" gesture. Jan rushed out to the car crying, "Paul, come quick—that lady is back!" We hurried back, but she was gone. When we get to heaven I sure want to know who that lady was!

❧

One of the greatest miracles of these next years of yet more testing and trials is the fact that TBN continued to explode with even more growth. TBN is, at this writing, seen on more than eighty TV stations in Russia, and a Russian satellite has just signed on the air! It is awesome to note that in 1993, when we celebrated our twentieth anniversary, TBN boasted 345 TV stations. Ten years later, on the eve of our thirtieth anniversary, the number has grown to over 4,000 stations, linked together by twenty-six great satellites!

Jan observed that the freeze the FCC had placed on new stations in the United States, as we shall see, was a blessing in disguise—it forced us to expand to many foreign nations. Without this deep valley I'm about to take you through, there might not have been *Hello World!* One thing I know for sure—Satan saw that his prize possession, RUSSIA, was being invaded after seventy years of spiritual darkness and night! Believe me, all HELL was aroused!

CHAPTER TWENTY-SIX

THE GATES OF HELL

SO HERE WE GO—BACK TO 1991. I LEARNED OF A bankrupt TV station that covered the great Philadelphia market. Channel 61 was being auctioned off by the bankruptcy court. "Are you interested?" asked the broker.

"You bet!" I responded. And so began an eight-year odyssey that would fill one hundred books.

By then, the new limit was twelve full-power stations and TBN was loaded. We not only had the full quota of twelve, but through a unique exception, the FCC had authorized an additional two stations if the corporation that owned them was *minority controlled*. Remember that word *controlled*—it's a dandy! Actually, TBN had formed a minority-controlled corporation several years earlier and had been applying for low-power stations (no limit) because the FCC gave preference to minority companies in order to encourage minority participation in TV broadcasting.

At first the company was called Translator TV, Inc., but when full-power stations in Midland, Texas, and Portland, Oregon, became available, we changed the name to National Minority TV, Inc. (NMTV). Jane Duff, an African American, had ably served for several years as one of my administrative assistants, so I asked her to serve as vice president, with myself as president. Reverend David Espinosa, an Hispanic brother and pastor, agreed to serve as the financial officer, so we had it—a minority-controlled board, two to one!

We had consulted with Colby May, our FCC attorney, and were advised that the corporation met the qualifications for the exception to twelve, i.e., fourteen TV stations in which, according to the policy, TBN could have a *"cognizable interest."* Remember this term also, as it is key.

NMTV had filed some years earlier and had been approved by the FCC to secure, as I said, Midland, Texas, and later Portland, Oregon. Everything was working just fine until—*Philadelphia!* Since TBN already had an ownership interest in the full fourteen stations, NMTV divested one station and virtually donated the Midland station to another Christian owner with an affiliation agreement to continue carrying most of TBN's programming. TBN, by virtue of my dual role as president of both TBN and NMTV, was now back to thirteen stations and ready to proceed with NMTV for Philadelphia—right?

WRONG! But I'm getting ahead of the story again!

❦

As things developed, NMTV was the successful bidder for the bankrupt station, WTGI-TV, Wilmington, Delaware, serving Philadelphia. We forwarded the purchase price—a bargain at $4 million dollars—and NMTV filed its application with the FCC. I remember turning in my Bible as I often do when faced with a major decision. It opened to Psalm 86. My eye went to verse 16:

> O turn unto me, and have mercy upon me; give thy strength unto thy servant, and save the son of thine handmaid.

What a good word of encouragement, I thought. *Surely we will have FCC approval soon.* But then I read the last verse, which said:

> Shew me a token for good; that they which hate me may see it, and be ashamed: because thou, LORD, hast holpen me, and comforted me. (Psalm 86:17)

Well, I knew we had many enemies, as the earlier chapters of this book surely confirm. I knew we would probably have some serious opposition to this great station covering the fourth largest market in the U.S. But I took this word to mean that the NMTV application would be approved and all enemies would be "ashamed" because the Lord would give us the victory—right?

Wrong again!

Only after eight long, agonizing years would I truly understand what God was speaking to me through this Scripture. Do not forget this word, as it was surely a word from the Lord and it was right on as we all will see at the end of this drama.

As we waited, Jan and I visited the station and met the staff. It was in a rented building in the heart of Philadelphia just down the street from the famous Liberty Bell; you know, the one with the crack in it. That, too, may have been a sign of trouble that was coming.

Most of the staff had already resigned or been laid off so there was only a handful of employees left. I am sure we will never know exactly who or why, but I do know that someone hatched a fiendish plot from hell to stop this station acquisition. A very evil person or persons reviewed the relationship between TBN and NMTV (National Minority TV), and came up with the theory that Paul Crouch had formed this phony front corporation, put a couple of ceremonial minorities on the board, and had abused the FCC policy by having control of more than twelve TV stations.

Sure enough, just such a theory and charge was filed by—you guessed it—a bunch of lawyers in Washington, D.C. Our attorneys answered every point of the numerous charges with records from the FCC, clearly showing that the Commission had thoroughly looked into the TBN-NMTV relationship and had duly approved it. We thought surely the FCC would simply dismiss such unfounded charges, but we were WRONG AGAIN! Bottom line: the FCC called us all in for an administrative hearing to discover the facts in this most unique case. December 1993—oh, God! This is where the nightmare begins in earnest!

❦

Those associated with the Philadelphia station had brought charges, hoping to stop NMTV from acquiring their station since, under the protection of the bankruptcy laws, they were doing just fine! Such abuse of the law is fairly common, as many creditors can attest! But now, sensing that both NMTV and TBN were facing disqualification charges, the "sharks" moved in. There was "*blood in the water*" and this prompted a feeding frenzy!

Another group filed a competing application against Channel 45, our station in Miami, whose license was up for renewal. Two minority advocacy groups filed petitions to deny our Miami license. This action would have been funny if the issue were not so serious. NMTV was actually doing the very work they advocated—namely, incorporating minorities into television broadcasting. But of course everyone knew, including the FCC, that these competing groups were primarily interested in just one thing: money! The hierarchy of those who craftily manipulate the law in this way is legalized extortion, plain and simple.

Finally, yet another party filed a competing application against Channel 40, our mother station in California. As I said earlier, the whole network was ultimately on the line.

Judge Joseph Chachkin, the Administrative Law Judge at the FCC, was all business. In these hearings they set you up front right next to his honor so he can look you in the eye as questions are fired at you by the attorneys. The whole procedure is about the same as a root canal without Novocaine!

For days, all of the principals and board members were questioned. Jane Duff, Pastor David Espinosa, Norm Juggert, and other staff members were interrogated. Also Pastor E. V. Hill, who had been added to the board of NMTV. All testified simply and truthfully that TBN, NMTV, and all of its officers and directors had understood that we were in full compliance with FCC rules and policy and were following the expert advice of our FCC counsel.

Finally, they were ready for the star witness—the mastermind who had "conspired" to circumvent the rules of this government agency—to abuse the policies of the Federal Communications Commission and control two more TV stations than entitled to— *Dr. Paul Franklin Crouch!*

CNN and other news agencies were there. They had asked the judge if they could videotape my testimony—he had agreed. So our attorneys demanded to do the same. The judge didn't like it, but he could hardly deny us the same right. When I got there, the courtroom looked a little like a presidential press conference! Hot lights, cameras, and action!

I was grilled by three sets of attorneys: the FCC lawyers, the group seeking our TV license, and the minority advocacy group attorneys. Of course, our own attorneys were there to object, counter, and defend me—God bless them!

The first day was fairly routine—a lot of history as to who, what, and when. Did I know this or that and when did I know it? All in all, it was pretty boring and everyone was glad when it was over. As I started to leave, my attorneys, Mr. Colby May and my new attorney, Mr. Howard Topel, warned me that CNN and other media were waiting for me out front. As I headed hastily for the side door, they spied me and came charging down the aisle to get their sound bite. Fortunately, I made it out the back door in time. As a result, my star performance did not even make the six o'clock news.

I have often counseled my TV ministry brothers never to give press interviews. They cut and paste your answers to make you look like a liar or a fool. If you refuse the interview, they have no story—so *don't ever talk to the secular media* is still my advice to all!

The next eight days were grueling. Lawyers are a breed all their own. They love to ask you a question many different ways to see if they can get you to contradict your first answer. After six or eight hours on the hot seat with his honor the judge staring deep into your eyes at your answers—well, you're ready for your own padded cell!

Finally, after probing my "gray matter" till it seemed there was nothing left, Judge Chachkin asked the question we all knew was coming. The lawyers call it the "smoking gun"! "Did you, Dr. Crouch, know that you were violating FCC rules and policy by exerting *de facto* control over the two NMTV television stations?"

My mind raced back over earlier testimony that had argued forcefully that the FCC did not have any written rules or policy as to how TBN should have conducted its business affairs with NMTV. In our application for the two stations our attorneys had always revealed that Paul Crouch was the president and was responsible for the management of NMTV like any CEO, but I was answerable to a minority board for all major corporate decisions. This very point was to be the life-or-death issue upon which this whole case turned, as we will shortly see.

"So, did Paul Crouch know . . . ?"

I took a deep breath, laid my hand on my Bible, looked

directly into the judge's eyes, and said, "Your honor, before God and with my hand on His Word, I declare to you and this court that I, at all times, followed the advice of our FCC counsel and believed at all times that I, TBN, and NMTV were in full compliance with all rules and policies of this agency."

A long pause, but now I read the judge's eyes—*he did not believe me*. I knew it in my heart. But now we would wait nearly *two years* for his initial decision.

During this time the lawyers for all parties went to work drawing up what the court defines as "Conclusions of Law and Findings of Fact." Naturally, each side puts their "spin" on everything, trying to convince the judge to rule in their favor. Our attorneys argued that the rules were not clear; nothing was written down, so how could TBN and NMTV have known what was in the Commission's mind? Therefore, TBN and NMTV should have all charges dismissed and all TV licenses renewed.

Of course, our opposition saw just the opposite. According to them, Crouch was a veteran TV broadcaster and he knew or certainly should have known. Mrs. Duff knew and everyone associated with NMTV, in fact, knew that they were deceiving the FCC. Therefore, TBN should lose Miami and all its other licenses in question.

Finally, the FCC lawyers who were technically the prosecutors in this hearing agreed mostly with TBN and NMTV. They concluded that, yes, the relationship was too close; and yes, Crouch had exercised *"de facto control"* over NMTV, but they agreed that the rules were simply not clear, so TBN should have its licenses renewed with, perhaps, a monetary forfeiture or fine.

❧

We rejoiced at the findings of the FCC staff attorneys and hoped against hope that Judge Chachkin would agree. *He did not!* On November 6, 1995, nearly two years after the FCC hearing, Judge Chachkin issued a forty-six-page decision that concluded:

> Accordingly, IT IS ORDERED that unless an appeal from this Initial Decision is taken by a party, or it is reviewed by the Commission on its own motion in accordance with Section 1.276 of the Rules of the FCC, the application of Glendale Broadcasting Company [our opposition] for a construction permit for a new TV station in Miami, Florida IS GRANTED; and the application of Trinity Broadcasting of Florida, Inc. for renewal of license of TV station WHFT (TV) Miami, Florida *IS DENIED*. [Emphasis added]

Have you ever received news so shocking that you felt like all the blood had just been drained from your body and the cold dew of death was clammy on your forehead? I pray, my children, you NEVER have to receive anything like this. I know many dear souls receive tragic news; for example, the death of a loved one. I do remember a similar shock when I learned of the death of my father as I recounted for you back in Chapter One. Well, I can tell you sincerely that this news was just as bad as the death of a loved one! For twenty years Jan and I had gone through hell and high water to see this fledgling TV network grow into a fine, strong voice. In a way it was like my own child. But now the gavel had fallen—a *death sentence* had been handed down. It felt like my life, too, had ended.

A very important lesson can be learned in tragic moments like this. Hear me, my children: Never make major decisions in the heat of emotional distress! The Word of God is clear:

> *Wait on the LORD: be of good courage, and he shall strengthen thine heart: wait, I say, on the LORD. (Psalm 27:14)*

That is very good advice, because when I finally got my breath back and my wits about me, far from giving up, I was ready to take some heads off! I was ready for *World War III!*

My ancestors were German and Swiss. Our most notable ancestor was Ulrich Zwingli, the contemporary reformer with Martin Luther. He died in a gun battle killing Catholics! Thank God we do not settle disputes like that anymore, but old *"Attila the Hun"* blood and genes are still there! Yes, my maternal grandfather was Lewis Zwingli!

After several days of just plain old shock, we all realized that something had to be done! We were not going to take this, as the old saying goes, lying down! For weeks we examined every possible strategy with our lawyers. We consulted with a minority lawyer who had been a former FCC commissioner. No one gave us much encouragement.

One idea that was suggested, I don't remember by whom, was to have Paul Crouch resign from the board. Since he was the "bad apple," maybe, just maybe, the FCC would overrule the judge and renew our licenses.

I remember that board meeting well! If it meant saving TBN, I was truly willing to step down. Jay Sekulow of the American Center of Law and Justice was willing to take over as president. But brace yourself, everybody, enter one more time: Annie Laurie Green's granddaughter, Janice Bethany Crouch! Once again, her Irish eyes were not smiling. *"Over my dead body will Paul Crouch resign from TBN!"* she exclaimed. With a few other expletives, that great lawyer-conceived idea went down in flames!

In the weeks that followed, another ominous turn of events occurred. The legal staff of the FCC that had tried our case did a 180-degree flip-flop! You remember, at the end of the hearing, they had pretty much sided with TBN—i.e., that the rules were not clear and our license should be renewed. Now, after the judge's decision, they hatched a whole new theory: Crouch had conspired with his FCC attorney, Colby May, and they together had conceived this clever ruse to circumvent the rules and policy of the FCC!

Now, Mr. May was a defendant who had earlier stepped down and had taken the witness stand to defend TBN and me. We will always be in Colby's debt, since many lawyers would have weaseled out and would have laid all the blame on Paul Crouch! Believe me, that took courage on Mr. May's part since now his attorney's license was also on the line!

For weeks, then months, the debate as to what action to take went on. Legally, we could file an application asking the FCC Review Board to review the decision. Not much hope there in the face of a full administrative law judge's decision. The other alternative was a petition straight to the full five-member Commission. Some of our attorneys were not optimistic. Their thinking was that we did not have a chance, since the FCC's Commissioners were all politically chosen, with a majority from the dominate political party in power, in this instance the liberal wing of the Democratic Party—these were the years of the Clinton Administration.

Rightly or wrongly, liberal Democrats believed that Christian television only supported conservative politicians and policies, so why should they help such "political opponents" by reversing a decision that hurt a group of Bible-thumping TV evangelists that were no friends of the Democrats politically?

As strange as this may sound, aside from this Miami nightmare, the Democrats have actually helped Christian television as much as all the Republicans put together! The "must carry" cable law is a prime example.

In 1992 Congress passed the "must carry" law. For several years the cable industry had been free to drop our full-power TV stations from carriage to make room for programs that brought in more money. This was the result of a court decision and was devastating to TBN and all the smaller TV stations. But the Democratic-controlled Congress at the time passed the "must carry" law only to be vetoed by President George Bush Sr. I wrote him an agonizing letter asking him, "How could you do this to us?"

He answered with an innocuous letter that made no sense to me. But then, wonder of wonders, the Democrat-controlled Congress overrode the Bush veto, giving us the Cable Consumer Protection and Competition Act of 1992! Presto, almost overnight TBN and its affiliates added about 20 million new households twenty-four hours a day! I still say God bless the Democrats for that! By the way, Senator Al Gore had led the fight for this bill in the Senate that became law. God bless him, too!

Naturally, the cable industry took the new law to court. For five years it worked its way up to the Supreme Court where, on March 31, 1997, it was ruled constitutional by a narrow five-to-four margin. May God bless the Supreme Court also—at least the five who supported the law!

Anyway, after months of consideration and debate, we came to the conclusion that a petition to the full five-member Commission was the next best step. I wanted to go straight to federal court, but the lawyers talked me out of it. It turned out that . . . but again, I'm getting ahead of the story.

❦

So, on the road again—papers, petitions, arguments, filings. One of the arguments noted in the record by NMTV was that Judge Joseph Chachkin was prejudiced against Christians and Christian television. Surprisingly, given the horrendous history of persecution the Jews have endured, Judge Chachkin, as a Jew, made some disparaging, condescending, and most revealing comments on the record during the trial. One of significant note was:

> It [TBN] was not just a religious broadcast service; it was to spread the [Christian] faith that Reverend Crouch professes.

Yes, your honor, and is that not what the First Amendment and Christian faith are all about? In my February 1996 newsletter, which

I hope he read, I said: "Be careful, your honor, there is a much higher Judge who will ultimately decide this case!" He also stated that Jane Duff, a beautiful, fairly light-skinned African American was—are you ready for this—"not Black enough"! Presumably "not Black" enough to be considered a true minority! Can you believe that the NAACP, who was one of our opponents, said nothing?

Finally, the FCC Review Board sent our final appeal to the eighth floor—the full five-member Commission. Nearly another three years would pass before a decision was handed down. Ah, the agony and the ecstasy of Christian television!

In the midst of this eight-year journey to and through the "gates of hell," Jan said that I "MUST" reveal two very clear temptations that Satan dangled in front of me. Ah, how subtle and clever he is! God even warns us that Satan often comes disguised as "an angel of light" (2 Corinthians 11:14)!

The first offer came from a group of—yes—Christian businessmen, headed by a well-known national leader. They had heard of TBN's and my dilemma and offered to come to our aid. They had—so the leader said—the millions of dollars we all believed it would take to settle and pay off all of our competitors. They would, then, hire the best law firm in the land to settle the issue with the FCC, and—praise God—TBN would be "FREE AGAIN"!

The condition—ready for a new one?—Paul Crouch and Jan Crouch would need to resign and cede total control of TBN to them! Of course, they hastened to say that Paul and Jan would be given "golden parachutes"—no, more like "platinum parachutes"— for this concession. And, of course, if Paul Crouch (the bad apple) was gone, the FCC would surely reinstate all of the TBN licenses!

We could actually name our price—within reason of course—but it was clear: Paul and Jan would never have to work another day of their lives and could, naturally, use the "windfall" to do many other good works of ministry wherever the Lord might lead!

The call honestly made me so angry, I think I saw "RED" again. But, upon reflection and prayer, I realized that if I judged these Christian brothers, I would be just as wrong as they were! Jesus said it clearly, "judge not"! So I must and shall always believe that their hearts and motives were pure and that they simply sought to rescue this great voice—TBN—from potential disaster.

When I refused, a second call came several months later, but as we shall see soon, this was surely NOT God's plan to save His TBN! My final answer was, "Hell will freeze over before I will sell TBN!" After that, the calls ceased.

The second temptation came from the world. I guess Satan figured if he couldn't get us with our Christian brothers, he would try with some really "BIG BUCKS"!

Mysteriously, an article appeared in the *Wall Street Journal* that TBN was being sold to another major TV network. This rumor went on to name a price: 1.2 BILLION DOLLARS! I instructed Colby May, our FCC attorney, to advise the newspaper reporter that no such deal was pending and that TBN was NOT for sale!

But the drama had just gotten started! A major New York brokerage firm specializing in the sale of TV stations had caught the newspaper story. They contacted us and begged us not to accept the alleged 1.2 billion, but let them have a crack at the sale. They offered to *start* the bidding at 1.9 BILLION DOLLARS!

Ah, dear children, I have been tempted many times and in

many different ways by the evil one, but I can assure you this was not one of them! I actually laughed at this offer and at the devil who surely inspired it. I instructed Terry Hickey, my administrative assistant, to advise this national firm that there was not enough money in the *whole world* to buy the TRINITY BROADCASTING NETWORK! The word eventually came back from several sources that Crouch was crazy not to sell because he was going to lose it all by an FCC decision anyway.

Actually, several Christian TV station owners have succumbed to the lure of huge financial offers. I grieve for every one of them. I wonder just how many souls we have lost for the Kingdom because Jesus was replaced by *LA Law.* I am sure the Judgment Seat of Christ will reveal many triumphs as well as many tragedies! I, for one, want to hear "Well done good and faithful servant" more than anything else I can think of.

So, to finally settle the question and crazy rumors that kept swirling around the country, I did something one day on the spur of the moment. My dear friend, Benny Hinn, was our guest on *Praise the Lord,* and I had recounted to him the allegation that TBN might be for sale. After a brief explanation I laid my right hand on his Bible there on the table and said to everyone, "I swear an oath before Almighty God that Paul Crouch will NEVER EVER sell YOUR TBN, Amen!"

By the way, Jan and I are working with our professional advisors to not only endow TBN, but to make it virtually impossible for future generations to sell TBN should Jesus tarry!

So, to my enemies, critics, and all heretic hunters who accuse me of wanting the partners' money, I say: WRONG AGAIN! Jan and I could legally have sold all the TV stations, kept the money in a nonprofit ministry corporation, and traveled the world on "missions" journeys, living like billionaires. But, at 65 and 69 years old, we are still going strong. I'm still building new stations, satellites, and networks. Jan is dreaming up hundreds of new programs to fill them up! Praise the Lord and ha, ha devil!

But back to our story. The full FCC final decision is just ahead.

As we waited for the Commission's decision, a bright spot appeared. Our opponents seeking our Miami and other licenses put forth feelers that they might be willing to accept a financial settlement to withdraw their competing applications. I suspected that this had been their motive all along. So we began negotiations through our attorneys to see just how deep the well was! To my astonishment the first number kicked around was something like $150 million dollars! Remember, the judge had actually awarded them our Miami license, so what was Miami worth to us if they withdrew?

By the way, another bit of good news came from Congress in the form of the Telecommunications Act of 1996. Shortly after the judge's decision, my attorney, Mr. May, and I assaulted Capitol Hill and poured out our horror story to a host of senators and congressmen. Newt Gingrich, then Speaker of the House, lent us a sympathetic ear and promised to help if he could. The result was a very good new law that prevents future extortioners from attacking us at license renewal time for "financial settlements"! In this case, God bless the Democrats, and the Republicans, and President Clinton for signing it.

Yes, thank God for this new safeguard for the future, but we still had this mountain to climb. With the prospect of a financial settlement I came to you, our faithful TBN partners, in the summer of 1997. We called it simply "The Save Your TBN-a-Thon"! I explained that if we could buy our competitors out, our attorneys felt it would help the Commission rule in our favor and reinstate our TV licenses. At least with no competitors we could go and talk to the Commissioners and lobby them in our favor. With competitors in the picture you cannot do that. It is called *ex parte* and is strictly illegal.

For five nights that July of 1997, Jan and I poured out our hearts to our faithful partners and viewers. We explained that while we did not know exactly how much it would take—we knew it would be many millions of dollars. They responded with far more than just financial pledges, but also overwhelming words of encouragement, advice, and prayers. The partners' outpouring alone could fill a book of its own, but this one from Betty Garey in Chattanooga, Tennessee, was classic:

> Last night was the first time I had heard why the additional money was needed for TBN. I am a single parent and work many long hours as both my sons are in college. When I heard you, Paul, last night, saw the weight on your shoulders, and felt the pain deep in my spirit, I knew the battle you had been going through. The scripture I wanted to call and give you was Deuteronomy 33:29: *"All your enemies will be found to be liars, and you will walk on high places."*

Betty went on to say: "The Lord is with you, fighting this battle for you, stand firm. Having done all—stand. You have the victory!"

Many had called in words of admonition as well. The consensus was that we should get down on our knees and literally pray for our enemies! That was hard for an old "Hun"—remember the German genes? But again, Betty's wise word was prophetic:

> Paul, your breakthrough came when you prayed from your heart for your enemies. That is when the Lord moved! Your heart was pure and in true humility you cried out to God for those who were persecuting you. God does not move contrary to His word. He commanded us to pray for those who persecute us . . . our enemies.

Yes, my children, we all learned many spiritual lessons from this long and arduous trial—one of the hardest was to truly forgive and then pray for our enemies. In a brief word, let me tell you how I came to terms with this. My cry to the Lord was "How can I pray blessing and prosperity on evil men who are literally robbing from *Your treasury?* HOW, GOD?"

And here is, I believe, a word of wisdom from the Holy Spirit. My prayer was to bless them, but not with material blessings. I prayed, "Dear God, send the Holy Spirit to them in mighty convicting power. Show them their error and SAVE THEM!" What greater blessing is there than salvation?

Another awesome word of prophecy came from our dear friend, Aquilla Nash, in Longview, Texas. She had called me early one Saturday just before our telethon. She said, "Paul, the Lord awakened me very early this morning and gave me a word for you. I do not fully understand it, but here is what God said: 'A ruling will be passed with a rider attached that will fully vindicate TBN and you.'" After a word of encouragement and a brief prayer, we said good-bye.

For days I thanked the Lord and Aquilla for this amazing word of the Lord. I took great comfort from it, which helped sustain me in the final rounds of this battle.

After the full week of "Save Your TBN-a-Thon," the wonderful partners had pledged about $65 million dollars—enough for me to continue serious talk of settlement. Surely God will reward those who gave sacrificially to save THEIR TV NETWORK! Their names have been inscribed in a book of honor that is sealed in a copper box and placed within the giant statue of Jesus on the white horse of Revelation. This great statue greets every visitor as he enters TCCI—Trinity Christian City International—at our new headquarters in Costa Mesa, California.

After many more months of agonizing negotiations we finally reached a financial settlement. The total number divided among four opponents was $65 million dollars! A breathtaking amount by any measure, but at least significantly down from the $150 million we began with!

So, armed with a settlement, we filed everything, as usual, with the FCC. Surely now the Commission would recant and the nightmare would end. Ah, my children, brace yourself once more. We're about to hit rock bottom as we pass THROUGH the gates of hell.

CHAPTER TWENTY-SEVEN

THROUGH THE GATES OF HELL

SO NOW OUR FATE RESTED IN THE HANDS OF FIVE FCC commissioners. As I said, nearly three years had passed since our final petition had been sent to the eighth floor. With the petition was our proposed "settlement" with our opponents, which also required Commission approval. The amount we had agreed upon was, as stated earlier, $65 million dollars! Surely now the Commissioners would feel we had been punished enough—*talk about a forfeiture or fine*—this was draconian and if approved, would make FCC settlement history!

The Commission, as I explained, was controlled by the Democratic Party since, at the time, Bill Clinton was president. The FCC Chairman was William Kennard, and the other two Democrats were Gloria Tristani and Susan Ness. The two Republicans were Michael Powell and Harold Furchtgott-Roth.

217

For several weeks we heard through our lawyers that a Commission decision was imminent. Oh, how we prayed! Many of our TBN partners and viewers joined us in intense fasting and prayer.

Finally, it came—of all days on April 15, 1999! The press release read as follows:

> Washington, D.C.—A deeply divided Federal Communications Commission issued a decision today denying the renewal of Trinity Broadcasting of Florida, Inc. for WHFT-TV, Miami, Florida. Trinity Broadcasting of Florida is an affiliate of the Trinity Broadcasting Network (TBN), the largest producer and distributor of inspirational Christian programming in the world. TBN and its affiliates are also the largest group owner of religious stations in the country with thirty full power, and hundreds of medium and low power television outlets.

☙

Devastating news, but an almost equal shocker was the decision that our competitors, Glendale Broadcasting, whom Judge Chachkin had awarded our Miami license to—WAS ALSO DENIED! The Commission cited misleading information, lack of candor, and a number of transgressions on Glendale's part. And if that wasn't enough, a third shocker—the FCC also denied the financial settlement we had signed with all of our competitors!

WOW! It took days just to assimilate all the decisions and to try and sort out just where it all left us! The bad news was: our Miami license was not renewed. It was sickening, devastating news. But there was some good news—our competitors had also been denied. So where did that leave our Miami station and license? That was unclear and yet to be determined. The final good news was that our financial settlement was also denied, and while the order didn't say so, it appeared that the Commission felt the amount was excessive. The order in turn encouraged the parties to resume negotiations and arrive at a new lower amount.

Now our final mission was at least clear—our only option was an appeal to the United States Court of Appeals, District of Columbia Circuit, Washington, D.C.

We also resumed negotiations with all of our competitors. The reason was simple. If we could buy out our competitors, they would also agree not to appeal to the federal court, leaving the issue solely with TBN Miami. After many rounds of consultation and negotiations, we arrived at a new lower figure—$44 million dollars divided among the four competing adversaries. I guess we can thank the FCC for at least reducing the amount of the settlement—by about $21 million dollars!

We can also thank Commissioners Michael Powell (Colin Powell's son) and Harold Furchtgott-Roth, the two Republican members. They voted to overturn the judge's decision and renew our Miami license. But the three Democrats were a majority and gave us the death penalty. Yes, my children, we have to forgive them, too, and even pray for them as well.

⚘

I'm sure they felt they were doing the right thing, but I could never understand one thing. Rupert Murdock, of the Fox TV network, had been charged with a far more serious violation. He was called on the carpet for a foreign ownership and control violation that was clearly defined in the FCC's ownership rules. He was let off with a mere hand slap and a fine. We had, at worst, violated a mere FCC policy, and one that was certainly not clearly defined, and we got the death penalty! Go figure that! I will always believe that someone, somewhere in the Clinton Administration did not like us—did not favor 100-percent-Christian television. But you can be sure that God will reward them one hundredfold and more!

So finally, we would have our version of the "Shoot Out at OK Corral"! We would finally have our day in court—the court of last resort: the U.S. Court of Appeals for the D.C. Circuit. Yes, there was yet the Supreme Court, but our attorneys advised that a dispute of this nature would probably never be heard by the Supreme Court, so here we went again—this time, for the last time!

So, my children, I'm sure you wondered as we all did at the time—what about all those words of encouragement, comfort, even words of prophecy? God was supposed to give us the victory! We were going to defeat all our enemies! They came at us in one direction but were to flee from us in seven directions! Had God failed us? Even worse, had we failed God so badly that He could not or would not defend us? These and many other dark thoughts would torment me for yet one more year.

Dear children, remember again the anointed advice that great saint of God, Paul Billheimer, gave us in his classic book, *Destined for the Throne*. In it he said: "Never accept an apparent defeat as final!"

So brace yourselves for one last great crusade. In the end we will see clearly why God in His infinite wisdom led us, yes, through the very gates of hell and back—oops, did I just tip my hand? You will see very soon now!

CHAPTER TWENTY-EIGHT

FREE AT LAST—FREE AT LAST!

THE FEDERAL COURT IS A FAR DIFFERENT ARENA from the FCC. First of all, it is not mired in politics and career bureaucrats who take their sweet old time, knowing they have tenure and compete job security. There is much debate on term limits for the politicians. I think there should be term limits for the bureaucrats! What took the FCC seven years to adjudicate took the federal court less than one year!

This was the "big leagues," so our attorney and fellow defendant, Colby May, felt that we needed a specialist lawyer—one who had experience in arguing cases before the three-judge panel of the U.S. Court of Appeals. After much research he recommended a veteran attorney, Mr. Timothy Dyk, who was—you guessed it—a Democrat!

I had some reservations—after all, the Democratic majority on the FCC had done it to us! Also, the judges who would hear our case had all been appointed by a Democratic president! But Mr. May's logic was "It takes one to know one"! When I finally met Mr. Dyk, I was convinced. He was a tall, distinguished gentleman who exuded courtly decorum. Besides, he had a quick wit and a sparkle in his eye that was captivating. By the way, attorney Dyk later became Judge Dyk, and now sits on the U.S. Court of Appeals for the Federal Circuit, Washington, D.C. Somehow I knew that we had found the perfect advocate to argue our case before the high court.

Once again, there were mountains of documents to review: Questions, questions, and more questions as Mr. Dyk buried himself in seven years' of FCC litigation! Most of this grueling work was for the lawyers, since my depositions and testimony were all "on the record." So was all the other witness testimony. Jan and my son, Matthew, had both given long and arduous depositions in spite of the fact that neither one had the faintest knowledge of the business affairs between TBN and NMTV. I suspected it was more busywork for the lawyers to keep the financial meter running!

Finally, the date for our trial was set: February 29, 2000. The year 2000 was a leap year, so our anniversary comes around only every four years! A few days before the trial we all met in Washington for a dress rehearsal. I vividly remember sitting at a huge, long table with all the lawyers who had been a part of our defense. There must have been twenty or more around that table as they conducted a mock trial. For most of that day the lawyers fired questions at Mr. Dyk—questions they knew the three-judge panel would ask. I answered a few questions to help him better understand some of the history of this tortured case that stretched back over seven long years. But mostly it was the lawyers who put Mr. Dyk through a grueling barrage of questions and objections, and more questions.

☞

In the end, our key argument was amazingly simple—it was the same, consistent argument we had advanced from the first time Mr. May responded to the FCC's initial inquiry concerning NMTV's proposed purchase of the Philadelphia station in 1991. The rules were not clear, the policy was not written down anywhere, so how could we be judged for some nebulous thinking in the minds of the FCC bureaucrats after the fact?

As it turned out, research had revealed several examples of case law where various government agency decisions had been overturned by the courts simply because they had not given the hapless defendants "CLEAR NOTICE" of what its rules and regulations meant and how they would be applied.

We had hit pay dirt! There was not one dissent among the lawyers that this was our key—"CLEAR NOTICE" become the hinge on our hoped-for door of release! I remember we all left that room with a strange feeling of exhilaration, even though most everyone gave us only a fifty-fifty chance of winning! God bless the lawyers—their "fifty-fifty" is a cop-out when they really don't know how a case will turn out. It's sort of like doctors who call everything they can't figure out a virus! We preachers are just as bad—when we have no answers we relegate it all to the sovereignty of God!

Finally the day arrived: February 29, 2000. Virtually all of the players were there who had been a part of this comedic tragedy! The FCC staff who had prosecuted our case and, yes, his honor Judge Joseph Chachkin was there to see if his historic decision would be upheld. Two whole rows were filled by our lawyers and supporters. I sat next to Colby May, whose future law practice was on the line, along with Miami and TBN!

Our advocate, Mr. Timothy Dyk, went first. After touching briefly on the history of our case, he went right to the heart of our argument. Not much history was necessary—it was clear that the justices of this high court had done their homework. They knew this case from beginning to end. Mr. Dyk went on to point out many case precedents where government agency decisions had been overturned for lack of *CLEAR NOTICE,* which was missing from their written rules or policies. The judges interrupted only a few times for a point of clarification, and our side rested. Each side had exactly fifteen minutes, but Mr. Dyk finished in about ten, graciously offering the extra time to the FCC attorney who was to argue against us!

Many of us were praying silently in the Spirit. I knew also that multitudes of our wonderful partners were also praying. I could literally feel the uplift and power of their prayers! Never forget, children: *"The effectual fervent prayer of a righteous man availeth much"* (James 5:16). I say again, that courtroom was charged with the exhilarating power of prayer—you could cut it with a knife!

Finally, the FCC lawyer stepped to the lectern. He appeared nervous as he opened his argument. Mr. May whispered to me that this was not the attorney he expected. The veteran FCC trial attorney had turned this case over to a young second-stringer! "Strange," Colby remarked.

The young man did his best, I'm sure, but never could get into a flow. He argued that Crouch should have known this and that. After all, Crouch was a veteran TV man and was well aware of FCC rules and regulations. The judges interrupted him several times, asking penetrating questions about the FCC rules and policies, and exactly how and where Crouch had violated them. The FCC lawyer could never quote a section or paragraph where TBN or anyone had clearly violated a written rule!

Finally, the chief judge interrupted the FCC lawyer and said, in essence, "Counselor, if the FCC did not give TBN clear notice as to the rules of this policy, your whole case collapses!"

❦

At those words, a shot of adrenaline hit the whole row I was sitting on! Furtive glances and smiles were exchanged by the lawyers and everyone! Colby May whispered something like "We got him!"

The young FCC lawyer struggled on for a while, but then the red light on the lectern came on, and in this court you sat down on "red" even if you were in the middle of a sentence.

It was over. We greeted all our friends and enemies as we exited. We even offered a hand of greeting to dear Judge Chachkin, who looked rather sheepish. The other FCC lawyers and staff allowed as how the case looked favorable to TBN. The press and reporters were all over the place, but Mr. Dyk severely cautioned me not to speak a word to them. We hurried to the elevator and beat a hasty retreat!

Yes, it was over; but again I was told we must wait—sixty, ninety, perhaps 120 days!

March and April passed. All we could report on the air was that our lawyers were cautiously optimistic as to the pending decision of the federal court.

As the Lord would have it, I was on a missions trip to India and China when the decision arrived. Remember this: never let trouble stop you or even slow you down on your mission from God! Remember the reply of Admiral David Farragut when he was advised that his ship would have to turn and run because torpedoes were coming at them. His response is legendary in American history books: "Damn the torpedoes, full speed ahead!" No, by God's grace, we never slackened our pace—TBN continued to grow and expand in spite of the "torpedoes."

Jan and I had joined Benny Hinn in Nairobi, Kenya, in April 2000 and rejoiced to see the fruit of our TV station there. Over one million had attended the great evangelistic crusade. We saw thousands confess Christ and many testified to instant healing as dear Benny ministered under a mighty anointing. At the end of the meeting Jan returned home with Benny's party, and Paul Jr. and I went on to India. I spoke to a huge gathering of about five hundred thousand people and rejoiced to learn that most of them were receiving TBN from satellite and cable TV.

It was May 5th as we sat down to a late dinner in our hotel when our cell phone rang. It was my chief administrative assistant, Terry Hickey. "Paul!" he shouted. "Awesome GOOD NEWS! The federal court just released its decision today! WE WON— THREE TO ZERO! Yes, a *unanimous* decision! The decision of the FCC is reversed, all licenses renewed, and best of all, the court VACATED the whole FCC record of our case!"

❦

That term, *"VACATED"* was not clear at the time, but when we finally understood what it meant, the plan of God, the prophetic word we had received, became crystal clear! I realized, finally, why God had allowed all the other doors to close. You see, if we had prevailed earlier at the FCC level, paid a fine or gotten a short-term renewal, for example, the record of this charge and proceeding would have *forever* been on our record to haunt us! But when the court VACATED the record, it meant the *whole file was removed as though it had never happened!* Sort of like "justification by faith." When a boy in Sunday School was asked by his teacher to define *justification,* the boy gave a classic answer we all still smile at: "I guess it means when God forgives you—well, it's just as if I never done it!"

Well, that is exactly what the federal court did for us. Suddenly I remembered dear Aquilla Nash's word of prophecy: *"A ruling will be passed with a rider attached . . ."* The court ruling overturning the FCC "death sentence" would have been joy unspeakable and full of glory all by itself, but to vacate the record was more than we could ever have hoped for! *"The rider attached"* was total and complete vindication for TBN, Paul Crouch, and Colby May!

Mr. May added yet another benefit to the decision. He explained that if TBN was ever in a competitive situation again, future enemies would surely dredge up the black mark on our record and use it against us. But now, that record was expunged—gone—never to hold us back in future dealings with the FCC! Apparently, the court felt that our treatment by the FCC was so egregious that they "vacated" or, to say it another way, completely expunged the eight-year record of this unique case. Of course, this is only my thought and perception of the verdict. This I know for sure—the U.S. Court of Appeals unanimously held in the written release:

> *Where, as here, the regulations and other policy statements*
> *[of the FCC] are unclear, where the petitioner's interpreta-*
> *tion is reasonable, and where the agency itself struggles to*
> *provide a definitive reading of the regulatory requirements,*
> *a regulated party is not "on notice" of the agency's ultimate*
> *interpretations of the regulation, and may not be punished.*

PRAISE BE TO THE LORD GOD MOST HIGH!

Jan actually got the news a day earlier, since it was May 6 in India when I received the phone call. Everyone wanted her to break in with a bulletin on TV, but she refused. She said, "This is Paul's victory—he should break the GOOD NEWS!"

God bless her—she knew better than anyone the agony I had uniquely endured, since the whole charge had been aimed at CEO Paul Crouch for supposed dereliction of duties in the business affairs of TBN and NMTV. So, thanks to my angel, Jan, I had the joy of standing under a Buddhist temple in Madras, India, and releasing the awesome news of our victory! We expressed the tape to TBN and Jan aired it only a few hours later.

Of course, it was also a complete vindication of Jane Duff, who had since been elevated to the office of president of NMTV during this crisis of uncertainty over the TV licenses of NMTV, as well as those of TBN. And don't forget Mr. Colby May. Remember, he stepped down as our attorney in this case to become a witness for the defense. He, too, was totally vindicated for giving his expert advice in the beginning. Mr. May continues, to this day, guiding the FCC affairs of TBN and our other affiliates.

But the good news did not stop with this monumental victory. Five days later, on May 10, the FCC granted our application, filed months earlier, to purchase twenty-four TV stations from our affiliate, All American TV. Eleven of these were full-power stations. Since TBN had been reduced to eleven stations, this action actually *doubled* our number of major full-power stations. Immediately this brought to mind a wonderful promise God had given us in back in 1998 from the prophet Isaiah. I had gone to London with Benny Hinn for a crusade at the world-famous Royal Albert Hall. I had asked Benny to pray and agree with us for the victory in this agonizing case. As we prayed, I opened my Bible and my eyes fell upon Isaiah 61:7:

> *For your shame ye shall have double; and for confusion they shall rejoice in their portion: therefore in their land* [TV land] *they shall possess the double: everlasting joy shall be unto them.*

The Scripture went on to say a word to our enemies:

For I the LORD love judgment, I hate robbery . . . (Isaiah 61:8)

Praise the Lord God most high! He crosses every "t" and dots every "i"! Only five days after our landmark victory, God gave us *EXACTLY DOUBLE* in our number of full-power stations, plus thirteen low-power stations for good measure! Yes, eleven new full-power TV stations from Honolulu, Hawaii, to Chattanooga, Tennessee; plus thirteen low-power stations sprinkled over the Midwest and Southern states! Praise God, the FCC was our friend again!

Yes, "Free at last, free at last! Thank God almighty," we were "free at last"! Of course, all the praise goes to our wonderful Lord and Savior Jesus Christ, because *"If the Son therefore shall make you free, ye shall be free indeed"* (John 8:36).

He was our GREAT ADVOCATE and He never loses a case! All praise to His holy name forever! Because of Him, this great voice called TRINITY BROADCASTING NETWORK would go on, free to preach the Gospel, free to sing His praises, free to GO, GO, GO into all the world with the glorious GOOD NEWS that Jesus saves, Jesus heals, and Jesus is coming again.

So, my dear children, there you have it. From the gates of hell to the very gates of heaven all in just eight years! Will there be more trials and tribulations? Yes, I'm sure there will be, but I can tell you this: we are all a lot tougher and wiser than we were eight years ago! All of us who went through that fiery furnace are battle scarred, but leaner and meaner than ever! I'm sure you are, too.

So, what's next? Read on, my children—my last chapter just may take your breath away!

EPILOGUE

SO, MY CHILDREN, WHERE DO WE GO FROM HERE? *Ah, this is where it gets really exciting!* So what were those first thirty years of testing, conflict, and technological explosion for? Was God calling us just to build a great Christian TV network for us North American, English-speaking souls? *Well—partly!* Was God wanting to show His mighty power to save and deliver His TV network from its many enemies? *Well, yes, but read on!* Would God have taken us through these deep waters, fiery trials, and *"lions' dens"* to reach only about 10 percent of the population of planet earth? *I think not!*

God tipped His hand a little bit with some of the technological breakthroughs that even we at TBN have experienced through the years. Remember our first "Holy Beamer"? The engineers said it was impossible to put a satellite uplink transmitter on an eighteen-wheeler semi-trailer truck! But we did it! Even in those early years of TBN we rolled the "Holy Beamer on the eighteen-wheeler" all over America, sending the great spiritual gatherings and conventions back to you, our TBN family. I will never forget visiting the executive offices of RCA Americom in Manhattan, New York City. On the president's paneled wall was a giant framed picture of TBN's new satellite uplink transmitter. The caption in bold print read: "TRINITY BROADCASTING NETWORK—THE HOLY BEAMER ON THE 18-WHEELER"!

We rejoiced as shortwave radio came on-line, sending the audio signal to the whole world in a twenty-four-hour period. Everyone was excited as God gave us cutting-edge technology with the new IPC, the International Production Center, in Irving, Texas, translating TBN programs into foreign languages. Next came the great facilities of TMC—Trinity Music City—in Nashville, Tennessee, with its Virtual Reality theater. Our pure, *high-definition TV* was years ahead of the FCC rollout of HDTV for broadcast television! Jan used the great church auditorium for serious TV dramas, complete with special effects and flying angels!

As we celebrated our 25th anniversary in 1998, we dedicated TCCI—Trinity Christian City International—in Costa Mesa, California. This state-of-the-art facility was originally the home of the Full Gospel Businessmen's Fellowship. When Demos Shakarian, the founder, went home to heaven, it was going to be sold, so TBN purchased it, Jan and company redid the décor, and I worked with the engineers in creating a futuristic, state-of-the-art TV production studio.

The truth is, technology is moving so fast that even the governmental regulators can't keep up with it! As I write this final chapter, we are consumed with the full-scale conversion from old-fashioned analog TV to the new HDTV—high-definition television. As usual, the whiz-kid inventors of new gadgets, bells, and whistles are so far ahead of us old fogies that I wonder if we will ever catch up! Remember the earlier quote from the book of Daniel:

> *O Daniel, shut up the words, and seal the book, even to the time of the end: many shall run to and fro, and knowledge shall be increased. (Daniel 12:4)*

My God—if I had ever wondered earlier if we are the generation that Daniel prophesied about—THAT ISSUE IS NOW SETTLED IN MY MIND AND SPIRIT! A blind man would have to SEE—*we are it!*

But if you think that all of the technological explosion we have seen and have even been a part of is awesome—you had better *buckle up!* No, that cliché is out of date. You had better don your 21st century SPACE SUIT and get ready to BLAST OFF! Indeed, if Jesus tarries, technology is moving so fast, God surely has plans for you, our next generation, that will make TBN look like Grandpa's old Model-T Ford! *Are you space suited up?* Okay, let's blast off!

How about an Internet computer that needs only an electrical hookup—the streaming video and other data comes in on the power wires? If that's not enough, how about an Internet wireless hookup where you can surf the Net while driving in your car, or—get this—walking down the street with the information screen—ready for this?—on the back of the lens of your eyeglasses! Pocket computers are already here. PDAs—personal digital assistants—are making access to "all the known knowledge of the world"—on the Internet—available to everyone with the click of a mouse!

The good news is simply this: someday you will be able to listen to or watch TBN *ANYWHERE* in the world—walking down the street, in your auto, at home—even flying in an airplane! I'm not sure about the astronauts, but you can be sure we'll get them, too!

For a little comic relief here, let me take you back many years to a thought that got everyone's attention. We know that TV signals travel at the same speed as light—186,000 miles per second. So we know that every TBN program ever broadcast is moving out into space. At this rate, the first *Praise the Lord* program that left earth in 1973 has barely reached the nearest star in our galaxy! I have teased us all for years that when we get to heaven with our new glorified bodies, and since we will be able to move at the speed of thought, we will be able to overtake all the TBN broadcasts and watch our reruns for eternity! I hope we can erase some of them!

But the real shocker—at least for the old-timers of my generation—is this one! Are you old enough to remember the Dick Tracy comic strip? Remember the wristwatch-sized TV screen and this master detective's ability to communicate everywhere in picture and sound? Well, believe it or not—it is coming!

But here is the ultimate of all time—I have read that scientists are dreaming that someday we won't even need a TV set or computer screen. You will simply connect electrodes to your head and—*presto*—virtual reality! In other words, looking at a TV screen will be passé. The viewer will actually have the sensation of *being in the picture*, not just looking at it!

But always remember, my children, for us these mind-boggling inventions are for one thing: *to win lost souls and bring them into the great Kingdom of God!*

Years ago, Jan's dear father, Edgar Bethany, used to say, "Children, put on your faith glasses." We could hardly understand this when we were trying to see even one TV station by faith! But today, even Papa Bethany's "faith glasses" are not needed—WE SEE IT!

Today, with all of the awesome technology at our disposal, we finally understand God's great master plan to reach every single soul on planet earth with the glorious Gospel of Jesus Christ! And together, we will not rest until those precious souls shall receive this message of salvation in their own cultures and languages through GOD'S MIRACLE OF TBN! Praise the Lord!

So, to all my dear children, and especially to my own sons, Paul and Matthew, I truly believe that this could be *the FINAL generation* that the prophets of old spoke of. I believe that before another thirty years have passed, we will all be rejoicing around the great throne of God! But if not, in a few short years I will pass the torch to YOU, and I am confident that you and even my children's children will carry this GOOD NEWS to the very ends of the EARTH! In that day you, too, will have no father but God.

I love you—Godspeed—Maranatha!

Sincerely,

Dad

P.S. I'm sure every father tries to instill wisdom and faith in his sons, but I am sure there are times when we wonder if the message is getting through. The following note was on a recent Father's Day card to me from my son Matthew. A message like this would make any father feel ten feet tall and that all of the investment in those growing-up years was worth it! I'm sure you will agree.

> *Dear Dad:*
>
> *Thanks for being a GREAT Dad. At about age 35 things change. You start seeing a larger picture. Life is not about yourself any longer. Dad has become wiser. Somehow ALL of the "life-lessons" that were automatically "blamed" on Dad become in focus, and the larger picture becomes "see-able." I'm not sure, but it's probably when you open the "spirit-eyes" that you really begin seeing for the first time. I'm starting to realize that what my life has been is ONE REAL BIG LESSON about "seeing by faith"! All I've known all my life is: "It is possible!" "God can do it!" After all the years of observing you, it's easy for me! Thank you from the bottom of my heart for teaching by example the greatest lesson a son ever has to learn. You're the best. The best is yet ahead.*
>
> *Love you,*
>
> *Matt*

P.P.S. At about eight or nine years of age, my eldest son, Paul Jr., composed the following poem that I think you will agree was mature beyond his years. This word of wisdom has brought many moments of joy to both Jan and me. We hope it will to you as well.

WHAT IS LOVE?
What is love? We really don't know.
Is it when your mommy fixes your toe?
Is it when you pray to God up above?
We still come to that same question, what is love?
Is it when you play football with your dad?
Or when your mom perks you up when you're sad?
When your mom spanks you and she looks very mad,
Really, inside, she's feeling very bad.
You always feel good when your dad is near.
We don't know what love is,
But we know it's here!
Paul Jr.

And further, by these, my son, be admonished: of making many books there is no end; and much study is a weariness of the flesh. Let us hear the conclusion of the whole matter: Fear God, and keep his commandments: for this is the whole duty of man. For God shall bring every work into judgment, with every secret thing, whether it be good, or whether it be evil (Ecclesiastes 12:12–14).